COCKERSAND ABBEY

A Lancashire House of Premonstratensian Canons, 1180-1539

Brian Marshall, B.A., M.Phil.

(Author of *Hackensall with Preesall; One thousand years of a Lancashire manor.*)

Landy Publishing
2001

The author, Brian Marshall, claims copyright in the text of this book. The terms of the Copyright, Designs & Patents Act 1988 and the Duration of Copyright & Rights in Performance Regulations 1995 are to be applied.

ISBN 1-872895-51-4

British Library in Cataloguing Publication Data.
A catalogue record of this book is available from the British Library.

Layout by Mike Clarke: 01254 395848
Printed by Nayler the Printer, Church, Accrington: 01254 234247

Published by **Landy Publishing**
3 Staining Rise, Staining, Blackpool, FY3 0BU
Tel/Fax: 01253 895678

Landy Publishing have also published:
Blackburn Tram Rides by Jim Halsall
A Blackburn Childhood in Wartime by Marjorie Clayton
Blackburn's Shops at the Turn of the Century by Matthew Cole
An Accrington Mixture edited by Bob Dobson
Rishton Remembered by Kathleen Broderick
Hell Under Haydock by Ian Winstanley
Wrigley's Writings by Bernard Wrigley
A History of Pilling by F. A. Sobee
A Century of Bentham by David Johnson
The Moorfield Pit Disaster by Harry Tootle
Bolland Forest & the Hodder Valley by Greenwood and Bolton
Sand Grown: the story of Lytham St. Annes by Kathleen Eyre

A full list of publications is available from Landy Publishing

PREFACE

Lancashire in the middle ages was a poor county; its agricultural potential was limited and its population was small. This was not an area in which great monastic houses might flourish, and none had been founded before the coming of the Normans. Wealthy Benedictine houses such as Ramsey Abbey with endless acres of wheat and barley, or Cistercian abbeys like Fountains, with vast sheep pastures, were never likely to appear in Lancashire's wet and boggy landscape. Nonetheless, thirteen monastic houses were founded within the shire, of which only Furness may be counted a major house, plus two others that were short-lived. There were also three friaries.

Cockersand Abbey, though gone for almost 500 years, still strikes a chord in the imagination of local folk. Close to its meagre remains a footpath brings people, particularly in the summer, to gaze at the chapter house and the few remnants of sandstone wall. Some strangers do not know what it is that they are looking at, while locals, a little better informed, often feel an affinity with this spot. It is for them somehow hallowed, its residents of long ago perhaps maintaining an ethereal presence. The Cockersand canons represented a significant spiritual, social and economic force in the region, and even today the site provides an evocative reminder of a long-ago community whose closeness can be sensed, just beyond the tangible.

The writing of this short book has been made easier by the assistance of a number of people. I should like to thank: Canon Frank Cookson of St. Bernard's, Knott End, and Messrs. Headlie Lawrenson and Richard Watson of Pilling for reading my manuscript and making many useful comments and suggestions. In particular I am indebted to Mr. Dennis Kellet of Thurnham, the owner and devoted custodian of the abbey site, who has given freely of his time and knowledge, not only to this work but also to countless members of the public who have visited the site.

I dedicate this book to my grandsons, Ben and Sam.

Brian Marshall

Brian Marshall,
Knott End-on-Sea,
February 2001

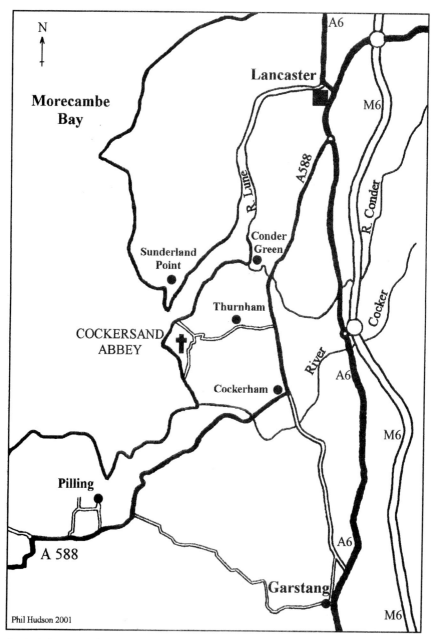

A sketch map showing the location of Cockersand Abbey in relation to neighbouring townships. Drawn by Phil Hudson, Settle.

THE BACKGROUND

Between 1534 and 1539 John Leland, chaplain and librarian to Henry VIII, journeyed about England on a commission from the king to list the holdings of monastic houses. This he did to good effect and as he proceeded he recorded many of his impressions of the monasteries he had visited. Of Cockersand Abbey he wrote that it was:

standing veri blekely and object to all wynddes

No words more apt than these have been used to describe Cockersand in almost 500 years that have elapsed since Leland wrote them.

Location

Cockersand is situated in Lancashire, on the shores of Morecambe Bay. It takes its name from the small River Cocker that bounds the manor of Cockerham to the south. The northern boundary of the manor is the River Conder that winds its way past the settlement of Conder Green and joins the tidal reach of the River Lune at the little port of Glasson Dock a short way up the Lune from the Abbey. Between Cocker and Conder the manor of Cockerham forms a promontory covering almost 6,000 acres, some of which is slightly elevated, fertile farmland. Part of it is low, flat, arable land that was peat bog until fairly recently, while much of the remainder is salt-marsh, subject to regular inundation by Morecambe Bay's high tides.

The site of the Abbey lies at the mouth of the River Lune where that river empties into Morecambe Bay. It looks across to Sunderland Point on the other side of the estuary, the great nuclear power stations of Heysham beyond, and the Lakeland hills in the far distance. Even at the beginning of the twenty-first century the visitor is reminded of Leland's words when the wind, unchecked, blows relentlessly across the flat farmland to the east or over the mudflats and sea by which this remote spot is bounded on the other three sides. In summer the site can be lonely, sometimes cold, and frequently subject to a wind that nags and annoys. In winter there is a starkness of chill and melancholy while the wind often reaches a force before which the few scattered thorn trees have long since bowed, and that sometimes threatens to blow the walker off his feet. In such conditions conversation can be conducted only by shouting. All the human being can think of is shelter; and there is none.

Looking north: beyond the chapter house can be seen the Lune estuary and the Nuclear Power Station at Heysham. On a clear day the Furness peninsula and Lakeland hills can be seen.

It is hard to imagine a spot less promising for human habitation – even today there are only a few farms and cottages scattered along miles of shoreline – yet it was here that a hermit by the name of Hugh Garth founded a hospital in the closing decades of the twelfth century.

The Growth of Monasticism

We know little of Hugh but the possibility exists that he was a member of, or at least connected with, the Premonstratensian order of Canons Regular which came into being in the early years of the twelfth century as part of the great monastic revival that was then taking place in Europe. Monasticism is almost as old as Christianity itself. It was a feature of the early Church in the Middle East, with individuals and communities believing that they could come closer to God by renouncing the world and establishing themselves in the deserts of Egypt, Palestine and Syria. In fourth century Egypt a number of men known as the Desert Fathers set standards for the future development of monastic practice that spread to Europe via Constantinople and Rome.

Two men in the early Church made major contributions to the growth of Christian monasticism, each by writing what has come to be called a rule. The earlier of these was Saint Augustine of Hippo, in North Africa, who lived from 354 to 430. He is famed for his writings, among which was a letter to a group of pious women that set out a model for the communal religious life. Although he was not a monk and did not seek to found a monastic order, this letter was to form the basis of what later became known as the Rule of Saint Augustine on which the life of many hundreds of monastic institutions was based.

The second of these two influential men was Benedict of Nursia, c.480-c.550. He produced a code for the organisation and conduct of religious communities that became known as the Rule of Saint Benedict, and was widely adopted by monastic groups. These 'Benedictine' communities that appeared throughout Europe – including the Anglo-Saxon kingdoms of Britain that were later to be known collectively as England – in the centuries following the saint's death, did not constitute a Benedictine order. They were independent houses broadly following the same rule. Though Augustine lived before Benedict, and his rule predates Benedict's, it was the latter who set the tone for early European monasticism. Augustine's rule was not to come to prominence until the eleventh century.

It was monks who first brought Christianity to the pagan English in the sixth century, though there were, in all probability, Christian communities still surviving, particularly in the North West, from Roman times. Augustine of Canterbury, himself a Benedictine, who came in 597 at the behest of Pope Gregory the Great, and Irish missionaries such as Columba and Aidan who entered England from the north at about the same time, established a church structured on monastic lines. This was particularly true of the Irish, or Celtic, church in which a bishop had no geographical diocese but exercised his episcopal function from a base in a monastery where he was subordinate to the abbot. The first Celtic house in England was at Lindisfarne which was quickly followed by others that included: Tynemouth, Gateshead, Lastingham, Hartlepool and Whitby. These monasteries were initially of the Irish type, with monks living in individual cells – probably beehive shaped – built close together. Further south, new monasteries following the Benedictine rule were established at such places as: Peterborough, Breedon in Leicestershire, Wokingham and Bermondsey in Surrey, and Hoo in Kent. Though other houses were established in Anglo-Saxon England, including large and wealthy ones such as Ramsey, Tavistock and Winchcombe, all of tenth century date, the number of pre- Norman Conquest houses remained small. In 1066 there were forty-eight monasteries in England, with a total of around 850 monks.

On the Continent, however, a new impetus had been given to monasticism some 150 years earlier by the establishing of a reforming movement at the abbey of Cluny in Burgundy in the year 910. No attempt was made at Cluny to change the Benedictine rule, but simply to enforce it, rigorously. This had the effect of creating 'Cluniac' houses in many parts of Europe, all subject to the Abbot of Cluny, and of galvanising into stricter observance of the Benedictine rule many of those houses that did not join the Cluniac movement. In Normandy, the duke and the barons founded religious houses as part of this upsurge of monastic zeal, and when they came to England they began to do the same in their newly conquered lands. William the Conqueror founded Battle Abbey and Selby Abbey, with his barons enthusiastically following suit, so that by 1100 the number of monasteries in England had risen to about 130, including the small Benedictine priory of Lancaster, created in 1094 by Roger of Poitou.

As the numbers of Benedictine houses increased under the stimulus received from Cluny, so several reforming groups appeared. The first of these non-Benedictine movements to emerge was that of the Canons Regular, or 'Augustinians' as they came to be known because of their adherence to the Rule of Saint Augustine. They were, strictly speaking, not monks, but groups of clergy living together under a rule, (regulus), and they became a major feature of European religious life from the eleventh century. Next came the Cistercians, founded in the late eleventh century by a breakaway group of Benedictines from the French abbey of Molesme. The new order believed itself to be following the Rule of Saint Benedict but soon came to be known as 'Cistercian' after its original settlement at Citeaux, sometimes called by its Roman name: Cistercium. Such was the appeal of the Cistercians, both to potential recruits and to the people at large, that within a few decades their houses were numbered in hundreds and their monks in thousands.

Premonstratensians

Yet another group came into being a few years after the Cistercians. This one was founded by Saint Norbert, a member of a noble German family, who in 1119, together with thirteen followers, went to Prémontré in eastern France, where he established a community of Canons Regular that observed with the utmost severity the principles and practices espoused by the Augustinians. The new body of canons quickly became a seperate order that was known by a number of names: 'Norbertines' after their founder, 'White Canons' after their dress, or 'Premonstratensians' after the place in which their order had its origins. They were formally recognised by the Pope in 1126.

The stream of new monasteries on the Continent quickly became a flood, with Cistercians, Augustinians and Premonstratensians vying with each other in piety and in claiming the support of the laity. These orders spread to England in the wake of the triumphant Normans and the number of religious houses in the country grew to something approaching 1,000. The Augustinians were the first non-Benedictine group to arrive when they established themselves at Colchester between 1093 and 1099. The first Cistercian house in England was founded at Waverly in Surrey, in 1128, while the Premonstratensians arrived at Newsham in Lincolnshire in 1143.

Monasticism in North Lancashire

Within thirty years of the founding by Roger of Poitou of the small Benedictine priory at Lancaster, another Benedictine house was established south of the Ribble at Penwortham. This was a small priory that was a cell of Evesham Abbey and never became independent. At Kersal, near Manchester, a small Cluniac cell was established around 1145. It was subject to Lenton Priory in Nottinghamshire.

The first of the new orders to set up a religious house in Lancashire was the short-lived order of Savigny which established, briefly, an abbey at Tulketh near Preston in 1124. It lasted only three years and the community of Savignac monks then abandoned the site to found Furness Abbey in 1127. In 1147, Furness, along with all other Savignac communities in England, was absorbed into the Cistercian order and quickly grew to become the largest and most influential religious house in the north-west of England.

Premonstratensian influence is apparent in the Lune Valley from around 1160. The Montbegon family gave land in Tunstall, Melling and Hornby to the newly founded Croxton Priory in Leicestershire, and at about the same date the small priory of Hornby was founded as a Premonstratensian house subject to Croxton. There was then, considerable awareness of, and regard for, Premonstratensians in North Lancashire, and it is no surprise that within a short space of time another house of the order was founded in the area, this time at the mouth of the Lune.

The Manor of Cockerham

In the middle of the twelfth century the manor lay within the lordship of William de Lancaster I, baron of Kendale and lord of Wyresdale, who c.1153 gave the manor of Cockerham, together with its church, to the Augustinian Abbey of Saint Mary of the Meadow, Leicester. The canons of Leicester regarded it as a valuable asset, although it lay at such a great distance from their house.

William died about 1170, and was succeeded by his son, William de Lancaster II, who revoked his father's gift to Leicester Abbey and settled Cockerham on his wife, Helloise, as dower. At a date between 1180 and 1184, William II introduced *"an heremyt of great perfecc'on"* by the name of Hugh Garth, to the site of Cockersand, within the manor of Cockerham, on the shore at the mouth of the River Lune. Hugh set up, evidently with the assistance of two 'canons', a hospital for lepers and other sick people, and was supported in this by charitable gifts. Only a few years after Hugh's arrival there was a Premonstratensian presence at the site. This is indicated by a document of June 1190 in which Pope Clement III referred to the Prior of the Hospital Monastery of Cockersand of the Premonstratensian Order. The Premonstratensians appeared so soon after Hugh's arrival that it is tempting to believe that the hermit was himself a member of the order, or at least in some way connected with it, particularly in view of its presence only a few miles away in the Lune Valley. Indeed, if his assistant canons were of the Premonstratensian Order then the likelihood is that Hugh also was a member of it. Before 1200 there is reference to an abbot, indicating a further elevation of status for the new foundation.

This rapid series of events was perceived by the abbot and canons of Leicester Abbey as violation of their title to the manor of Cockerham. It had reposed in their possession for more than three decades and now, not only had it been taken away from them, but a rival religious house had been set up within its boundaries. William de Lancaster II had died around 1184, but Leicester Abbey went to law against his widow, Helloise, and her new husband, Hugh de Moreville, demanding the restoration of its Cockerham estate. Though the details of the law suit and the dates of particular events are somewhat vague, it is clear that the abbot and canons of Leicester had a strong case, and the newly arrived Premonstratensians at Cockersand were on the point of abandoning their fledgling foundation as legally untenable. Indeed, it appears that they may well have done so.

Theobald Walter and the Manor of Pilling

The group of Premonstratensian canons, precariously placed, both legally and domestically, on the windswept shore at Cockersand, passed at this point into the protection of Theobald Walter, brother of Hubert, Archbishop of Canterbury, lord of Amounderness and progenitor of the wealthy and influential Butler family of Lancashire and Ireland. With the canons ready to abandon the Cockersand site, Walter made arrangements for their accommodation elsewhere. Before 1200 we find some of them at Pilling, Cockerham's neighbouring manor, and a few possibly at Tuam in County Galway, Ireland. Walter was a man of great wealth and influence in England and Ireland and such arrangements would have been easy for him to make. Pilling was one of his own manors while Tuam lay within the lands of his friend, William de Burgh.

The case in favour of Leicester Abbey, and against the Premonstratensians, was strong and it appears that the move was meant to be permanent, with the monastery, initially to be built at Cockersand, to be built at Pilling instead. This seems to have been the intention of Theobald Walter when he gave the manor, or hay, of Pilling to the canons. Significantly, he gave it to them, not when they were at Cockersand, but when they were at Pilling, and the wording of the charter contains no mention of Cockersand:

> *dedi et concessi et hac carta mea confirmavi totam hayam meam de pylin deo et beatae Mariae et abbati et canonicis praemon-stratensis ordinis ibidem deo servientibus in puram et pertpetuam elemosinam ad unam habitiam edificandam de ordine praemonstratensi*
>
> *I have given and granted and by this my charter confirmed all my hay of Pilling to God and the Blessed Mary and the abbot and canons of the Premonstratensian order serving God in that very place, in pure and perpetual alms for the building of a house of the Premonstaratensian order*

Almost without exception, charters giving land to monasteries name the house concerned, and the absence of a reference to Cockersand in a charter as important as this one supports the view that the canons were not at Cockersand but at Pilling, and that the abbey was to be built at Pilling. This argument hinges on the Latin word, *ibidem*, which means: in that very place; just there; or, in the same place. Since no place other than Pilling is mentioned, the only possible conclusion is that Pilling was the intended site.

The first abbot of whom we know was Thomas, named in a document dated between 1194 and 1199 as *Abbas de Marisco*, (Abbot of the Marsh), who was probably the abbot referred to in Walter's charter. Another abbot, Roger, probably successor to Thomas, is also said to be Abbot of the Marsh, though in 1205-6 he is referred to as, *Abbas de Kokersand*. It is telling that these early abbots are said to be 'of the Marsh', for the marsh in question is unlikely to have been Thurnham Moss, by which the Cockersand site is surrounded on the landward side. Mosses were not, and are not, normally referred to as marshes. The word is customarily applied to the salt-marsh that is regularly covered by the higher tides, and of this there is an abundance in the area of the ancient chapel of Pilling, while there is little of it in the immediate vicinity of Cockersand. Furthermore, we must ask why Roger is referred to firstly as 'Abbot of the Marsh' and then at a later date as 'Abbot of Cockersand'. Had he been domiciled in the same place during the whole of his abbacy there would have been no need to use these two different titles. This argument is complicated a little by the use, in a document of 1206 or earlier, of the phrase: *Canonicis beatae Mariae de Marisco super Kokersond*: (the canons of the Blessed Mary of the Marsh upon Cockersand). Such a phrase suggests that the marsh in question could, in fact, have been at Cockersand. On the other hand it could indicate that the canons of the Blessed Mary of the Marsh were now at Cockersand having recently returned there.

Since the abbot and canons moved to Pilling before Theobald Walter gave it to them we might consider where it was intended that they should lodge, Pilling being a place as remote and desolate as Cockersand. The canons constructed a grange at Pilling from which to run the manor as their '*demesne estate*', or home farm, the site of which – now Pilling Hall Farm – is close to the ancient chapel of Pilling, and it is pertinent to ask if the chapel was already there, together with a parsonage, in which a few canons from Cockersand might have found a temporary refuge during their dispute with Leicester Abbey. The chapel was small, and so too would have been the priest's house, which possibly accounts for why it was necessary for some of the canons to go to Ireland rather than to Pilling.

Theobald Walter recognised the plight of the newly arrived contingent of canons and offered them, not only a temporary place of residence in his Pilling manor, but also an alternative site for their new abbey should their litigation with Leicester Abbey fail to confirm them in the Cockersand site. They did, of course, return to

Pilling Hall Farm. The house is on the site of the grange built by the Cockersand canons around 1200. The stone is millstone grit, similar in colour to that found in the abbey ruins and probably quarried at Parkside Farm, Conder Green.

Cockersand but we do not know, and may never know, whether or not they actually started to build their abbey at Pilling. Their grange was in being within a very short time and it may be that the building that was intended to be the abbey became a mere grange instead.

We are unable to assign a date to the original chapel at Pilling. It was abandoned in the early eighteenth century for the church now known as the 'Old Church', and though the location, at Newer's Wood, is well known, nothing now shows above ground. An excavation by the Pilling Historical Society in 1952 revealed sandstone and also some millstone grit – both evidently from Cockersand – and foundations of rough boulders. The church was shown to have had a semi-circular apse at its east end, and a bead of Anglo-Saxon type was also discoverd at the site. The apse is a feature of many Anglo-Saxon churches and this, together with the boulder foundations, could indicate a date considerably earlier than the Norman-Conquest. Further detailed examination is needed in order to learn more of the chapel's early history, and go some way towards explaining just why – if in fact it does predate the arrival of the Premonstratensians – a church was built in so inaccessible a spot at so early a date. Although as holders of the manor, the church at Pilling belonged to the Cockersand canons, there is no reference to the building of it, by them or anyone else. If they did not build it we must suppose that it was already there when they first appeared on the scene between 1190 and 1200. Also of considerable interest would be the excavation of nearby mounds which could prove to be the remains of the priest's house.

The Pilling chapel site is on a small island formed by the conjoining of drainage dykes. Such a configuration of man-made waterways is not accidental and was evidently done in order to provide a moated area, perhaps for defensive purposes. No record of such intent survives and only archaeology might tell us anything about the construction of this mysterious little church. Does its origin lie in a period when north-west England was part of a troubled frontier region, perhaps as early as when the area formed part the post-Roman kingdom of Rheged, or later when the northern kingdoms, first Strathclyde, and then Scotland, were laying claim to it? Or might it have some affinity with Saint Patrick's chapel at Heysham where Irish influence is thought to have been present as early as the eighth century?

Compromise is Reached

The legal dispute between Cockersand and Leicester was eventually resolved by restoring the manor of Cockerham to the canons of Leicester and completely detaching the Cockersand site from the manor, thus allowing the new Premonstratensian foundation to continue in being. The site of the abbey is small, and the legal agreement made it clear that the Cockersand canons were to have nothing in the way of land or other resources from the manor of Cockerham. Such an agreement indicates the vital importance to the new religious house of Theobald Walter's gift of Pilling. By 1207 the abbot of Leicester had sent several of his Augustinian canons to establish a small priory at Cockerham, to safeguard the interests of Leicester Abbey against the burgeoning influence of the newcomers at Cockersand. Cockerham Priory and Cockersand Abbey remained uneasy neighbours for 270 years.

Cockerham Priory was never an independent house, remaining a cell of Leicester Abbey and never occupied by more than three or four canons, one of whom was the prior. It was centred on the parish church which stood where today's nineteenth century building stands. There are no remains to be seen and we cannot be sure where the canons lived, although nearby Cockerham Hall is the most likely place. The one remaining feature of the priory is its fishpond, or at least part of it, which is situated in the pasture across the road from the hall.

Premonstratensian Popularity

The original Premonstratensian canons at Cockersand came from Croxton Abbey in Leicestershire, a house founded less than thirty years earlier, and much favoured by landholders in the Lune Valley. Such was the regard in which the order was held at that time that recruitment levels were high, and Croxton, new as it was, would have had little trouble in finding a dozen canons to go off to the Lancashire coast and set up a new house in such spartan surroundings.

Piety and devotion of the kind displayed by the Premonstratensians appealed greatly to the population at large, and recruits flocked to the order. Only thirty years after its foundation, the heads of a hundred Premonstratensian houses attended the General Chapter of the order at Prémontré. Equally, it attracted extensive endowments in land, churches and property from wealthy benefactors who were keen to have such a group working on behalf of their immortal souls. At a time when men believed that their sufferings in Purgatory could be shortened, or avoided altogether, through the prayers and intercession of holy men, the Premonstratensians seemed highly suited for the purpose. Who better to intercede with God than men living in self-imposed misery and squalor in order to demonstrate their devotion to Jesus Christ and their disdain for worldly goods? A simple tunic, rarely changed or washed so that it teemed with vermin; a frugal diet and living quarters that lacked every amenity but the most basic; no underwear or hose, despite the worst of the weather, and a fortitude born of unswerving faith in God; these were the practices and qualities that brought the White Canons a popularity they could never have imagined or sought at the time Norbert established the first house at Prémontré.

By the third decade of the twelfth century there were two distinct groups of canons regular: the austere Premonstratensians with their houses in remote and often uncomfortable locations, and the Augustinians who interpreted the Rule in a much more liberal fashion, and did not impose upon themselves the excesses of zeal so avidly pursued and endured by their Premonstratensian counterparts. The distinction between the two groups can readily be seen within the manor of Cockerham itself where it is clearly reflected in the choice of sites for the two houses. Cockerham Priory, standing serenely amid meadow and pasture, with its small church and a pleasant hall with private bedchambers where the canons lived in uncloistered ease, is very much the sort of place where we might expect to find a small community of Augustinians(Black Canons) caring for the local people as both lords of the manor and parish clergy. No more than two miles away, Cockersand Abbey, grim, exposed and solitary, was a place where life lacked any comfort, or relief from the unrelenting elements, and where the inmates might, in a moment of pride, flatter themselves that theirs was the higher calling and the stronger vocation.

The tide of monastic fervour swept across Europe, and eventually saw the founding of monastic houses in places on the very edge of settled England. Its most distant and faintest ripples brought it to a wild and lonely spot on the shores of Morecambe Bay, where the seed, no matter how unpromising the ground in which it was planted, took root, and Cockersand Abbey, though never wealthy or grand, maintained its position against wind, waves, plague, marauding Scots and the vagaries of economic fortune for 350 years, and in 1539 was the last of the Lancashire monasteries to be dissolved.

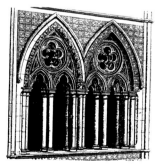

Thirteenth century triforium arcade; a feature that may have been lacking at Cockersand since there were evidently no aisles.

THE SITE AND BUILDINGS

The Site

Inland of the Cockersand site the land today is flat – arable and pasture – with only an odd hillock here and there rising much above sea level. This area is still known as Thurnham Moss, for such it once was. When Hugh set up his hospital, and the canons of Croxton arrived in their new abode, the hinterland was a peat bog, stretching to the hamlet of Thurnham that stands on a low hill some two miles away. Such a bog, or moss, would have provided fuel for the canons, in the form of peat – known locally as 'turf' – when cut and dried, but was impassable in many places and presented such a bar to movement that communication with the outside world was best maintained by boats, plying the Lune to Lancaster, or larger vessels that visited the abbey's possessions on the rivers Wyre, Ribble and Mersey further south

It is interesting to observe that the place where the abbey came to be built had about it an aura of sanctity even before the hermit took up his abode there, which was perhaps what brought him to the spot. This piece of land was known as the site of Askell's Cross: a cross presumably erected by a man called Askell. Such a name is of Scandinavian origin and would have been common enough around Morecambe Bay. Just what the purpose of the cross might have been is not clear. Wayside crosses were plentiful in the middle ages, throughout Lancashire and England in general, but they were usually to be found on highways, sometimes on lesser roads, and at crossroads and boundaries. There may have been a roadway, or path, out on the bleak shoreline beyond Thurnham Moss. Such a road would have followed the firmest ground from the Lune to the Wyre: along the natural embankment that occurs in many places and, where no embankment exists, across the salt-marsh when tide permitted. It is possible that Askell placed his cross to mark a spot along this road that was for some reason already regarded as holy.

Another very good reason for building the abbey where it now stands, and for returning to Cockersand from Pilling, is the local sandstone. The spot may well have been sacred but it is also on top of good quality sandstone which is not immediately apparent today as it lies below the pasture. This sandstone forms the underlying stratum, or bedrock, across much of the area. In a few places, particularly at Cockersand, it is close to the surface and can be seen outcropping on the shore. It was readily available, it required no transportation, and above all, it was free.

The abbey stood on a low eminence at the very edge of the seashore. The land is protected from the tide by a natural embankment which has been given a stone facing in modern times against which the waves lap, or pound, according to the mood of the elements. In earlier times the bank itself would have been subject to constant erosion. With the sea to its front and the bog to its rear the potential for development of the abbey was limited to this relatively small elevated area. The impression that the site was actually an island must often have been given, with the windswept sea driving against the bank and the bog encroaching closely on the other side. Indeed, it evidently was an island at times as was graphically illustrated on 17 March 1907 when a great wave swept over the embankment on both sides of the site and flooded the area to the rear, causing the abbey ruins to stand isolated from the mainland until the waters subsided. Local folk at the time declared that this was not uncommon as, 'the sea comes back once every fifty years to claim its own again.'

Although there is evidence of other material, chiefly millstone-grit, in later phases of building at Cockersand, the greater part of the structure, was of the local sandstone, the earliest phases exclusively so. The durable millstone was evidently used in the later fourteenth century on more elaborate details, such as mouldings and tracery, higher up in the church tower. The most likely source of this stone is some three miles from the abbey in a quarry at Parkside Farm, near Conder Green. It is close to the tidal reach of the River Conder and stone could conveniently have been carried in shallow boats or on rafts down the river at high water and round to the abbey landing stage.

The Buildings and Contents

Once the canons had arrived at Cockersand, and were certain that they were going to stay, building could not have been delayed. No matter how hardy and pious they might have been, living accommodation for themselves would have had to be a high priority. The most urgent task was the quarrying and cutting of the local sandstone into suitable building blocks. Then there was the problem of obtaining lime from which to make mortar. This will have had to be brought in from the beginning as none is available locally. A likely source for it is the Carnforth area where it would probably have been obtained already processed into lime rather than as limestone. It would then have been carted the short distance to the sea and brought down the coast to Cockersand.

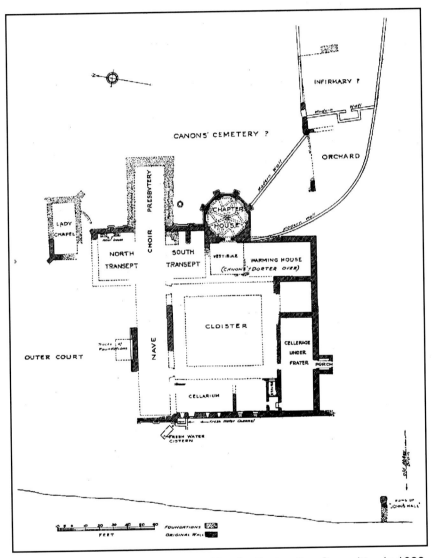

Ground plan of the abbey as revealed by the Exploration Committee in 1923. Reproduced by permission of the Lancashire and Cheshire Antiquarian Society.

A structure vital to the Cockersand community throughout its existence on that remote shore was a pier or jetty, or some kind of landing stage to allow the regular passage of goods and people in and out of the site. Accustomed as we are to the roads and railways of today it is perhaps hard to imagine the difficulties encountered in overland transportation in the thirteenth century. Even where roads existed, and where there was no wide expanse of quaking peat bog, the passage of wheeled vehicles or pack-horses was painfully slow, if it was possible at all. The bringing of goods or building materials overland to Cockersand would have been a lengthy and extremely tedious process, and in the case of millstone-grit for building, probably impossible because of the sheer weight of it. By sea, almost anything could be brought conveniently to the very door of the abbey. A landing stage would have stood high and dry at low tide, but at high water, vessels could be berthed and cargoes loaded or discharged with relative ease. Good evidence for the use of seagoing vessels as a means of reaching the abbey is provided in a document of March 1497 when Richard Redman, Abbot of Shap, was arranging a visit to Cockersand. He instructed that an experienced man be sent to Lancaster on the 2nd. of April, to meet him and conduct him safely among the dangers of the sea to the abbey.

Building Commences

The canons themselves would have participated in the manual work during the first phases of building, but they can have numbered no more than a dozen in the early days, and considerable hired help would have been necessary. The central feature of any monastic establishment is its church, and the Cockersand canons would have wanted their church as much as they needed shelter for themselves from the wind and rain. It is possible, therefore, that the earliest work was on the south transept of the church together with a building adjoining to the south that later became the north-eastern part of the cloister range. In this way they could have provided a chapel in the transept for their daily round of offices and masses, and accommodation for themselves in the ground floor of the other building. As work progressed they added an upper floor which became the permanent *dorter* for the canons. From this upper floor a night stair would have led down into the south transept so that the canons could enter the church conveniently for those services that took place during the night, and afterwards return to their sleeping quarters. Such a stair was a feature common to most monasteries. Having housed themselves the canons could then proceed with work on the church.

The Abbey Church

The ground plan, revealed by the work of the Cockersand Abbey Exploration Committee during August and September, 1923, shows a cruciform church of considerable size, being some 175 feet in length and over 70 feet across the transept. The nave was about 100 feet in length and the chancel 45 feet. Nave and chancel had an interior measurement of some twenty feet across. In comparison, Whalley Abbey, laid out on a site less limited than that of Cockersand, and with a larger monastic community in mind, had a church similar in size to Ripon Cathedral at 260 feet in length. If, however, we compare the church at Cockersand with some churches still to be seen in the area we become aware of just how impressive a building this must have been. Lancaster Priory Church, at 170 feet is of similar length, Saint Helen's, Churchtown, a church belonging to Cockersand for over three centuries, and in the building of which the canons were closely involved, is forty feet shorter at 130 feet. Pilling, a township that belonged to Cockersand for 340 years, now has two churches: one of early eighteenth century date which measures some 70 feet in length, while the magnificent late nineteenth century church, designed by Paley and Austin and visible for many miles in all directions, is around 135 feet. All these churches, however, are much wider than the Cockersand church appears to have been, a dimension produced in most of them by the addition of side aisles. Premonstratensian monastery churches generally had at least one side aisle; many of them had two, and it is the apparent absence of aisles at Cockersand that causes the church plan to be so narrow. It is possible, though, that there was at least one aisle, which investigation has not shown, and that the church was a good deal wider than the revealed ground plan would seem to suggest.

We have no means of knowing how high the church stood, nor what it might have looked like, except by comparison with surviving fragments of other Premonstratensian buildings in various parts of the country. It is evident, from scattered masonry identified on the site, that work was going on during the Perpendicular period of architectural style which lasted from the later fourteenth century to around the mid-sixteenth; that is from about two centuries after Cockersand was founded to the time of its destruction. There was a tower such as we see in many churches of the period which was probably situated in the conventional place: on the crossing. It has been suggested that the tower was located on the west front, like that of Shap Abbey, another Premonstratensian house. At Shap, however, the tower was built around 1500 by Abbot Richard Redman in keeping with the fashion for west towers on monastery churches in the late fifteenth and early sixteenth centuries. Similar, though unfinished, towers of this date may be seen on the church of the Cistercian abbey of Holm Cultram in Cumberland and on the Augustinian Bolton Priory in Yorkshire. There is no evidence of building going on at Cockersand at so late a date and the tower is more likely, therefore, to have been on the crossing. Wherever it was, it evidently had crenellations, or battlements, as indicated by masonry fragments, and was topped by a steeple, which, like that on the present church at Pilling, would have been a magnificent landmark. The likelihood is that the Perpendicular work represents a raising of the height of the church, when the incumbent abbot felt that such extension could be afforded.

The Great Inventory

Much detail on the abbey and its contents and property comes from the great inventory of monastic houses taken on the orders of Henry VIII in 1536. The commissioners who visited Cockersand were: Sir Thomas Langton, Sir Henry Farington and Sir Thomas Southworth, all Lancashire knights, with Thomas Burgoyne as auditor and Thomas Armer as receiver. They passed systematically through the buildings, recording and valuing what they found, and their findings tell us a great deal, not only about the goods and chattels, but also about the buildings. It is in this survey that we find reference to the church steeple, something that examination of the ruins could never have told us. The commissioners were not so much concerned with the steeple as with the lead used on it for flashing and guttering. This, with lead from some of the abbey's other buildings weighed more than twenty tons and was valued at £66 13s. 4d.. In addition, the six bells in the steeple, together with the sanctus bell, were valued at £60.

Local tradition has it that the Cockersand bells now hang in the belfry of Cockerham church, a suggestion with which the architect John Swarbrick, a member of the 1923 Cockersand Exploration Committee, found it difficult to agree, unless they had been melted down and re-cast. The present writer's grandmother, born no more than a mile from the abbey, often repeated the local tale that the bells had been taken to Cockerham from Cockersand by Oliver Cromwell. Given that country folk in the nineteenth century would have known of Oliver Cromwell and had probably never heard of Thomas Cromwell, the architect of monastic destruction a century before Oliver's time, it is interesting that a name so appropriate as Cromwell crops up in this piece of folklore among people who otherwise knew little or nothing of what had gone on at Cockersand four centuries earlier.

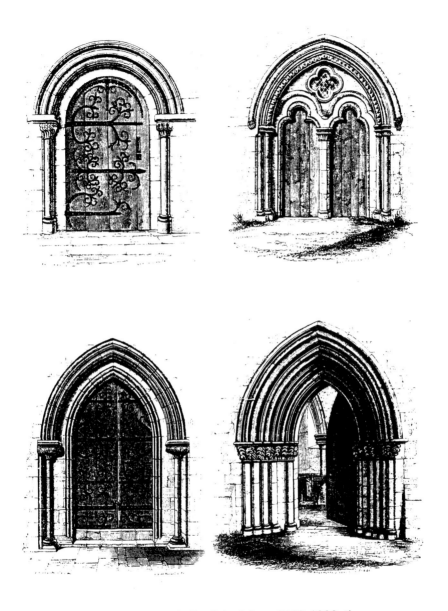

Doors in the Early English style, c.1200-1300, the
period in which Cockersand was built.

Inside the Church

The church interior would have been light and was well endowed with the customary ornamentation. In the chancel alone were nine windows containing an estimated 216 square feet of glass while in the nave were eleven windows containing 200 square feet. A common feature of medieval churches was the lady chapel, often placed at the extreme eastern end of the church building, beyond the chancel. At Cockersand, however, the lady chapel appears to have been a small detached building close to the end of the north transept, from which there was direct access. The high altar in the church was of carved wood. It is described as having 'imagerye', and was estimated in 1536 to have been worth forty shillings. There were five chapels in the church, each with an alabaster table as an altar, collectively valued at forty shillings, and another altar of alabaster in the lady chapel. Since most of the canons in residence were ordained priests these altars would have been in regular use for all to say their daily masses. Yet another chapel in the church is described as the 'abbot's chapel, well wrought and carved,' and valued at forty shillings.

Other items listed in the church included, a chalice and paten(communion plate) of silver, weighing fourteen ounces and valued at 3s. 6d. per ounce, a total of £2 9s. 0d.; a pair of silver censers weighing twenty-eight ounces at 3s. 4d. per ounce: £4 13s. 4d.. There was a considerable collection of vestments and altar linen together with two chests behind the altar, presumably for storing the vestments. Beside the altar stood a seat for the abbot that was valued at twenty pence. Two great candlesticks of brass stood in the chancel and there was one of iron that was hanging. These were jointly valued at two shillings and eightpence. Also hanging in the chancel was a brass lamp, doubtless the sanctuary lamp, which was reckoned at tenpence.

A wooden lectern with an eagle on it was valued at one shilling, while the thirty stalls in the choir for the canons were reckoned to be worth £3 6s. 8d.. The exquisite choir stalls to be seen in Lancaster Priory Church are said by some to have come from Cockersand Abbey. Can it be that these are the same stalls as those valued by hard-headed Lancashire landowners in 1536 at a little over two shillings each? Also in the choir were fifty-four books of parchment, valued at exactly the same price as the thirty stalls. As Swarbrick points out, though, the value estimated by the commissioners was what they considered a realistic sale price – given that the likely market was among local people – and not a figure determined by craftsmanship or aesthetic perception.

Of particular interest is a small ivory box, said to be used as the pyx which is not described but is likely to have been carved, and was valued at eightpence.

The Cloister and the Chambers

A major feature of monasteries is the cloister, an arcade or covered walkway arranged around a square court or garden where the monks or canons could exercise, even in inclement weather, and where work of various kinds such as manuscript copying and illumination could be carried on in good light. The customary place for the cloister was in the right angle formed by the transept and nave of the church. Some occur on the north side of the church but most are to be found on the south, in order to obtain the greatest benefit from the sun. This was the case at Cockersand where a faint suggestion of the square can be discerned in the turf by the imaginative visitor.

In a tight, unbroken square around the cloister stood the main monastery buildings, two storeys high. The commissioners passed through these buildings, room by room, recording everything they found there and estimating its value. The compartments they listed are as follows: Dorter, Library, Abbot's Chamber, Abbot's Bedchamber, Sea Wall Chamber, Inner Chamber, Hey High Chamber, Under Chamber, Middle Chamber, End Chamber, Hall, Buttery, Pantry, Kitchen, Abbot's Dining Chamber, Abbot's Buttery, House Under The Abbot's Chamber, Bread House, Bakehouse, Brewhouse, Bolting House, Farmary, Chapter House, Cloister, Frater, Jordan Chamber, Kilnhouse. Many of these are sleeping quarters for the canons, servants of various types and pensioners or others living on the charity of the abbey, and the items listed in them consist mainly of bedding: mattresses, blankets and the like. Bedding appears to have been given a relatively high value. For example, in the abbot's bedchamber was a feather bed valued at 6s. 8d., a mattress at 1s. 8d. two blankets at 1s. 8d. the pair, a quilt at 1s. 8d., a coverlet at one shilling and a pillow at fourpence. The abbot's bedding then, was valued at something like six of the choir stalls. There would, of course, have been a ready market for bedding, while buyers for intricately carved choir stalls would have been hard to find. There was also some fairly basic furniture distributed through the various chambers, much of which was not regarded as being of any great value. For instance, in the Sea Wall Chamber was a table, a cupboard, two chairs and a form, collectively valued at four shillings.

Some of the rooms were for a specific purpose and the items listed in them reflect such uses. In the Kitchen, for instance, are listed: pots, pans, skillets, ladles and the like, while the Brewhouse had vats and tubs for the brewing of ale, the staple drink of the canons. The Bolting House was a small room set aside for the sifting of flour, the Kiln House for the drying of corn. The Frater, or canons' dining room, was sparsely furnished with trestle tables and benches; the Farmery, or

The afternoon sun lights up the interior of the chapter house allowing us to see the fine central column with its decorative frieze. To the right of the door may be seen fragments of worked stone from the abbey church.

A thirteenth century decorative arch surrounds a nineteenth century funerary monument of the Dalton family from nearby Thurnham Hall.
Photos loaned by the Art Dept., Ripley St. Thomas School, Lancaster.

infirmary, was similarly furnished. The Jordan Chamber contained a limited amount of furniture and its function is not made clear in the survey. The name evidently came from Jordan of Bosedon, abbot of Cockersand c.1354-64.

It is of interest to speculate as to why a room in an abbey should have been named after one of its abbots. Did Abbot Jordan endear himself to the monastic community at Cockersand in such a way that the canons forever afterwards revered his memory? Such an act on his part might well have been the setting up of a warming room. This was an institution common to houses of the order which the canons might enter for brief periods in order to gain some little comfort in the depths of winter. Apart from the kitchen it would have been the only room in the abbey to have any artificial warmth in it. At Cockersand in particular the canons would have had good reason to be grateful to an abbot who inaugurated such a facility on their behalf, and would no doubt have blessed his memory whenever they came into it from the bitter cold of a January day

The Cloister was paved with small tiles and had twenty-one windows, each with an area of eighteen square feet of glass, valued in total at £3 3s. 0d.. There were also ten stalls or seats valued at one shilling each. In the Library no furniture was recorded but there were fifty-two books, collectively valued at five shillings, with a further fifty-four, valued at 6s. 8d., in an aumbrey on the side of the Cloister. The wording of the inventory is not altogether clear but presumably it means that the aumbrey was accessible from both Library and Cloister. The book collection in the Library numbered one hundred and six books which, together with a further fifty-four in the choir made a total of a hundred and sixty. This was an impressive figure, even for a community of canons who could all be expected to have been literate, and is thought to have been one of the largest collections in Lancashire.

The Chapter House

Finally, we consider the Chapter House, the only building on the site to have survived in any recognisable form. Such a building was an important feature of monastic establishments, being the place where regular meetings of the community were held to discuss the business of the house. The abbot normally presided, with the canons seated around the walls, sometimes on chairs, or stalls, often on stone seats built into the structure. The latter was evidently the case at Cockersand since the commissioners have listed no furniture of any kind except a great aumbrey which they valued at eightpence, and in which, presumably, reposed the collection of grants and charters that have survived to tell us so much about the abbey. The Cockersand Chapter House is constructed in the Early English style. It dates from around 1230, and stood at the end of the south transept backing onto the building on the east side of the Cloister. Access was from a vestibule below the canons' dorter. The building we see now is flat on the west side where it adjoined the cloister range, and also on part of its north side where it was joined to the south transept, with a matching face to the south side. The east side of the Chapter House has three angled faces with buttresses at the angles. In its present form the interior is dark with the open door in the west wall being the only means of admitting light. The commissioners, however, found five windows – long ago walled up – each with fifty square feet of glass, which would have given good light.

Despite its outward shape, the Chapter House at Cockersand has an octagonal interior, the only one of its kind in an English Premonstratensian house. Many houses of the order had a rectangular chapter house. The one that survives at Cockersand, or its interior at least, is evidently of early thirteenth century date and is probably the original. The roof is supported by a central column from which radiates a pleasing arrangement of vaulting ribs. From the early nineteenth century the Cockersand Chapter House was used as a mausoleum by the Dalton family of Thurnham Hall, the owners of the site. More than twenty members of the family are said to lie buried beneath the floor, the level of which has been raised considerably to accommodate these interments. This raising of the floor level accounts for the apparent absence of the stone seats for the canons. The present floor is some three to four feet higher than the original, and the seats, now buried, remain in their original position. If the visitor can imagine a floor three or four feet below the present one, the whole scene within the chapter house changes. A fine ornamental frieze around the central column, and other embellishments on the walls, now below shoulder height, become two or three feet above the head; where the builder intended them to be, and the roof, now accessible to the touch, is lofty and out of reach.

Windows are recorded by the commissioners in many of the rooms, with some, like those in the church and the chapter house, being of considerable size. Plate glass such as we see in windows of today was not known and windows were customarily made up of small panels arranged in lattice formation. Such panels might be square, or they might be diamond shaped pieces known as quarries. Though plain, or white, glass was known, most windows, certainly those in churches, had painted or coloured glass in them, and this would have been the case at Cockersand, reducing to some extent the light that might otherwise have been admitted. These small glass panels were, of course, re-usable which is why the commissioners placed a value on all the windows. No doubt they were among the first items to find a buyer when the abbey was dissolved three years later. Iron bars are listed at almost every window where they formed the framework into which the small glass panels were fitted. The strength and rigidity of iron bars, rather than lead strips, would have been needed at Cockerstand to withstand the full force of the westerly gales to which it was so often exposed.

Water and Drainage

A significant problem to be considered would have been the provision of fresh water for cooking and brewing, though since this was a Premonstratensian house little would have been used on laundry and personal hygiene. Many monastic houses, of all orders, were built alongside running streams from which a channel could be cut and led through the establishment to be used for all the usual domestic purposes including the flushing of the *reredorter* before being taken back into the main stream further down its course. If no suitable stream existed a well or series of wells could normally be sunk. There was no stream at Cockersand, however, and wells sunk so close to the sea would produce water that was brackish at best. The community, therefore, was dependent on rainwater, a commodity that would normally be in regular supply at this site. In the course of its excavation the Exploration Committee of 1923 identified a fresh water cistern below the west wall at the junction of the church and the cloister range, with a channel leading to it along the side of the building. This highlights the importance of maintaining the guttering in good order and justifies the use of the large quantities of lead that we have noted. Where the rainwater runoff could not conveniently be directed to the cistern we may suppose that water butts were strategically placed to catch as much water as possible.

It is, of course, likely that wells were sunk by the canons. A well of apparently early date in the yard of nearby Abbey Farm may well have supplied water, mostly for purposes other than human consumption: watering livestock and flushing drains and latrines for example.

There was a main drain which emptied through the embankment to the south-west of the abbey site, either onto the shingle beach or into the sea, depending on the state of the tide. This would have been quite hygienic as no matter what was deposited it would have been quickly removed by the sea. Even the drain outlet itself would have received a regular scouring from the higher tides. Anthony Hewitson in his book, 'Northwards,' published in 1900, states that there was an opening in the embankment in front of the ruins and that in 1881 a man had made an inward exploration of some forty or fifty yards. The man found the passage blocked with sand and, reporting nothing of interest, concluded that this passage

Outlet of the main drain in the sea wall; now bricked up. The drain leads under the abbey site and probably gave rise to the stories of an underground passage. Photographed in 1983 by Dennis Kellet, owner of the site.

must be the main abbey drain. Hewitson also states that human bones are sometimes found on the shore, having been washed through the drain by heavy rain. This is highly likely as there must, over the centuries, have been many hundreds of burials on the limited area occupied by the abbey and its immediate environs.

Secret Passages

The drain, and the story of a man progressing along it for some distance, will have contributed to the belief among local folk that there was a subterranean passage running from Cockersand Abbey to Thurnham Hall. There is also a story that a similar passage ran, not only underground but also under the sea: from the abbey to its grange at Pilling. The first of these passages would be a little over two miles in length while the second would be a good three miles. Underground passage myths are common throughout the country and frequently take no account of major problems of civil engineering and ventilation such as the supposed Cockersand passages would entail. Perhaps even more importantly, they rarely advance a reason for constructing such passages.

The buildings of Cockersand Abbey, with its church steeple dominating, were a familiar sight for more than three centuries. From the sea and from inland the abbey was the most prominent structure to be seen in the area. Mariners entering the bay would have used it as a landmark for the Lune channel and overland travellers passing along the highway from Cockerham to Lancaster would have remarked its sandstone walls standing, remote and vulnerable, on the very edge of the sea.

Elegant piscina, c.1250. The communion wine and water were probably kept in one such as this beside the high altar at Cockersand.

ESTATES AND PROPERTIES

The medieval monastic movement was like nothing that exists today. We could dismiss it as a great confidence trick played upon a gullible population by groups of monks who were bent on an easy life, and for their own ends cynically exploited the superstitions of the people. On the other hand we might see it as the monks claimed it to be: a bastion against the spiritual enemies of the world. The power of evil was perceived as being just as real as the power of an enemy country and, like the soldiers needed to fight against a human foe, soldiers were necessary to defend against the even more dangerous enemy that threatened the soul. Monasteries existed for the purpose of prayer, and those men and women who forsook the world to live in them did so in order to pit their combined strength against the evil that sought constantly to take over the world. They were the front-line troops, and their weapon was prayer, directed unceasingly, day and night, to God, who, provided that he received constant and devout supplication, would protect the world against the great enemy.

Gifts of Land

Most monasteries were founded by lay magnates, usually men of noble or royal status, who provided a suitable site together with endowments in land for the upkeep of the monks. The founder would invite a prior or abbot from the order of his choice to send a group of monks or canons, usually thirteen in number – a figure that symbolised Christ and his twelve apostles – to set up the new house. Such a benefaction on the part of the original donor was granted to the monks under a form of tenure known as *frankalmoign*. There were several forms of land tenure at this time, knight service being the best known of them. Under this form the tenant was required to present himself, or a substitute, as an armoured and mounted soldier – a knight in fact – whenever the feudal army was mustered. Other forms of tenure required rent or services of some kind from the tenant. The monks, however, were required to provide nothing except prayer. A man who set up a new monastery and provided land for the monks, expected that they would pray daily for his soul for ever; long after his death and that of the monks he brought in to start the process. He expected that, centuries later, he would still be gaining spiritual benefit from his original act of charity, and indeed the monks at their daily masses and their endless round of other services prayed for: 'our benefactors living and dead.' Belief in Purgatory lay behind such a practice. A person whose soul languished in this place, intermediate between Heaven and Hell, could gain an early release from his ordeal through the prayers and intercession of others, and monks, men in the forefront of the spiritual battle, were regarded as the ones best suited to provide these on his behalf.

A new monastery then, was expected to provide spiritual aid for its founder, and usually also for others in the area who took advantage of this opportunity to gain salvation for their own souls. Local landholders, great and small, began to give pieces of land, in frankalmoign, to the monks, and in many cases a religious house could find itself, within a decade or two, in possession of extensive estates. Some abbeys, founded in the Anglo-Saxon period already held substantial lands but after the Norman Conquest the process was accelerated so that by the fifteenth century perhaps as much as one third of land in England may have been held by the monasteries and churches collectively.

Typical of the kind of major grant made to monasteries was Theobald Walter's donation of Pilling Hay, that is the whole manor of Pilling, some 6,060 acres, to the abbot and canons of Cockersand with no expectation of anything other than prayers for his soul. King John gave Little Singleton, 1194 acres, on exactly the same terms, and the de Hackensall family similarly gave more than 1500 acres in Preesall.

Many of these grants have survived and show that the donors indicated what they expected by means of a simple formula. Most declare that the land is being given: *in puram et perpetuam elemosinam*, (in pure and perpetual alms), and that its purpose is: *pro salute animae meae*, (for the health of my soul). It was also common for a donor to invoke the mercy of God, through the prayers of the monks, on behalf of others, usually named members of his family such as his wife, children or parents. Sometimes we find one that is all encompassing: *pro salute animae meae et animarum omnium antecessorum et successorum meorum*, (for the health of my soul and the souls of all my ancestors and descendants). That is, on behalf of some people not yet born, and of others long ago dead.

Land in Lancashire

In the Lancashire hundred of Amounderness alone, huge amounts of land were given to monasteries of one kind or another. Cockersand held more than 12,500 acres of Amounderness land; Whalley Abbey held the manors of Staining, Hardhorn and Newton, amounting to 5,260 acres; Lytham Priory, a cell of Durham Cathedral Priory, held 6,242 acres; the Cheshire abbey of Vale Royal held the manor of Kirkham, some 857 acres; and the abbey of Dieulacres in Staffordshire held over

3,820 acres in what is now Fleetwood, Thornton and Bispham. The total area of land in Amounderness held by monasteries was over 36,000 acres or about 23% of all land in the hundred.

Cockersand Abbey held land in all six of the Lancashire hundreds, often referred to as shires, as well as in Cheshire, Yorkshire, Cumberland and Westmorland, all donated by landholders seeking to procure salvation for their eternal souls. For example, in the hundred of Salford, or Salfordshire, the manor of Westhoughton, an area of 4,341 acres, was given to the abbey in the middle of the thirteenth century. In Leylandshire, the hundred south of the Ribble, Cockersand's holdings included Tarleton with Holmes, 5,534 acres, and Hutton, 2,744 acres. The areas of these three manors alone when added to that of Amounderness bring the total of the few holdings we have so far considered to more than 25,000 acres. Tarleton with Holmes, though the largest of these three manors, was the least productive, yielding in 1537 only £9 9s. 3d. in rents. Westhoughton did only a little better with £10 9s. 0d., while Hutton, smallest of the three, produced £26 9s. 2d.. The largest manor was the least productive because it was mainly moss. Peat, or turf, was of little use except as fuel when dried. Only Hutton, smallest of the three manors, was producing income to match its potential. This was, and remains, a fertile area, for which reason the first Lancashire Agricultural College was established there in the twentieth century.

Land was given to monasteries not only by royalty and nobility but also by men, and women, of lesser stature. Such people were the holders of small manors, or parts of manors. They were largely untitled people, of no particular wealth or standing, whom we might call the 'minor gentry'. Anyone who held title to land under some form of feudal tenancy could donate all or part of it to another, and many did so. A wealthy man such as the king, or Theobald Walter, could give a manor or two to an abbey and think little of it, but others had to be more circumspect in their charity. The de Hackensall family of Preesall, for example, held Preesall with Hackensall, Hambleton, and some parcels of land in a few other manors. They were not in the same class as Theobald Walter but they gave about one third of their Preesall estate to Cockersand. They could hardly have given more and still maintained a reasonable level of income. Those even further down the scale, freemen with small holdings, could not manage anything so extensive as this but they gave: an oxgang (probably about fifteen acres) here, an acre there, half an acre, a croft, a toft, or small pieces of land measured in a dozen different ways. A very familiar donation was of a strip of land in the common field of the manor. These strips, still widely to be seen in pastures throughout Lancashire, particularly in the Fylde, are often called *sellions* in the charters. Also frequently occurring in the charters are grants of land whose size we cannot calculate because they refer to markers and boundaries of which today we know nothing. A typical charter of this type might read: 'all my land from the oak tree to the cross by the highway thence along the stream to the land held by Thomas.' Clearly we have no means of knowing where such a piece of land might lie, let alone its extent.

In West Derby, the most southerly Lancashire hundred, there were large numbers of small grants of land made to Cockersand in the first half of the thirteenth century. Donations were made in thirty-five townships: Melling, Maghull, Allerton, Knowsley, Kirkdale, Rainford and Orrell, for example. None amounted to a whole manor though some were of several oxgangs, and many were of areas defined in such a way that we cannot calculate their extent.

The hundred of Lonsdale produced grants of land in fifty manors, with smaller numbers in Blackburnshire and Salfordshire, and there were donations as far away as the city of York, northern Cumberland, along the upper Lune in Westmorland, and in Cheshire. It would be extremely difficult to calculate the total area of the lands held by Cockersand Abbey, and we may be certain that it was not a figure that the abbot and canons would have known with any certainty. We have already seen a figure in excess of 25,000 acres in respect of the abbey's holdings in Amounderness, together with two manors in Leylandshire and one in Salfordshire. Perhaps we would not be too much in error if we considered a modest 10,000 acres for the sum of the remainder, and something over 35,000 for the total.

Land Donation Comes to an End

The charters by which these donations were made were recorded in a Chartulary compiled by Robert de Lachford, one of the Cockersand canons, some time between 1268 and 1280. Most of the donations will have been included in Robert's work as little was given after his time. The practice of donating land to monasteries came, more or less, to an end in the reign of Edward I as a result of a number of statutes. The first of these was the *Statute of Mortmain* of 1279, which required anyone holding land directly of the king to obtain royal licence before alienating any of it. Next came Edward's second *Statute of Westminster*, 1285, which empowered a donor, or his heirs, to reclaim land given to a monastery if such land had been further alienated by the recipient community. Potential donors might still have been willing to give land under this condition though such gifts were made a little less attractive to monastic communities as a result of it. The third statute was the most critical in bringing about a cessation of land alienations to monasteries. This was the *Statute of Quia Emptores*, 1290, which sought to retain the king's right to services from his feudal vassals. If, for example, a feudal tenant of the king owed knight service for a piece of land and gave that land to a monastery, the obligation to provide an armoured knight was to be assumed by the monastery. This passing on of the obligation with the land was to apply, whatever kind of service or rent was involved. After this the monasteries, reluctant to find themselves providing services for the king, were generally unwilling to accept donations of land.

Chantries

The belief in the efficacy of prayer for the souls of both living and dead continued, and a way for wealthy men to continue obtaining it was quickly found. This was in the form of the chantries: small individual chapels, either within existing churches, or built seperately, where one or more priests would be employed to pray and say masses exclusively for the proprietor and those nominated by him. Such chantry priests were simply paid a stipend by the patron and no grant of land need be involved, though in some cases, chantries did accumulate small estates through minor donations. Cockersand Abbey served two such chantries, at Tunstall and Middleton in the Lune Valley, by providing priests who were canons of the abbey. The canons were sent out from Cockersand and resided at the chantry where they were known as *custos* or warden, or *cantator*, which means singer or chanter.

The two chantries presided over by Cockersand canons are typical of those to be found throughout the country. That at Middleton was founded by Sir Edmund Neville in 1337. He used one third of the manor of Middleton to provide funds for the building of the chantry, for its maintenance and for the stipend of a Cockersand canon who was to say daily masses there for the Neville family. The last canon to hold the position was John Preston who, if he was still alive, would have been 63 years of age when the chantries, like the monasteries before them, were suppressed in 1547. The Tunstall chantry was endowed by Thomas de Tunstall in 1397. It was originally in the parish church but was at some point transferred by the Tunstall family to their home at Thurland Castle. The last canon to officiate there was Abraham Clitheroe who received a stipend of £6 per annum. Clitheroe was 59 years old when the chantries were abolished.

The extensive lands acquired by Cockersand Abbey during the thirteenth century might, had they been in another part of the country, have had great potential for the creation of wealth for the abbey community. Unfortunately, much of Lancashire, in which county the greater part of the land lay, had little to offer the cultivator since it was regarded as of poor quality and vast areas of it were nothing more than undrained peat bog. In the first half of the eighteenth century, two hundred years after Cockersand Abbey had been dissolved, Gervase Markham wrote:

*Lancashire is one of the most barren counties in England, a country
more backward agriculturally than most countries in Europe.*

The fertile and productive agricultural landscape that we see in Lancashire today is a product of a later period. It was not there for Markham to see and it was certainly not in being when Cockersand Abbey held so much land in the county.

Management of the Estates

When a monastic house received donations of land on the scale that Cockersand experienced it was necessary to make decisions as to how it was to be managed to the best possible advantage. The great majority of pieces of land could not be cultivated by the abbey as part of its own scheme or policy. Acres, half acres, crofts, strips and any other small areas were simply left in the hands of their tenants who then paid the rent and dues to the abbey instead of to the former owner. Even larger areas such as two or three oxgangs, unless they were situated adjacent to large estates of the abbey, would be left with the tenant at a suitable rent. It was the collection of these rents, many hundreds of small sums, and various payments in kind, such as honey and chickens, that occupied some of the abbey's agents through the year over an area stretching from Carlisle to Chester and from York to the Irish Sea. These small amounts, often no more than a few pennies, were vital to the abbey's economy. Sections of Cockersand accounts for the years 1251 and 1260 have survived and may be seen in Volume III, Part III of the Cockersand Chartulary. They list large numbers of tenants, each paying a small amount, and illustrate very clearly the abbey's dependence on the rents derived from these minor landholdings. Only large areas such as whole manors, like Pilling, Hutton, Medlar, Westhoughton and Little Singleton, would be run by the abbey as seperate enterprises.

In the case of a whole manor, or large estate, the abbey would set up a grange from which to run it like any other medieval manor. The word grange means, barn, and such they were: storage places for the produce of the estate pending sale, or transportation back to the abbey. The grange also included accommodation for two or three lay-brothers from the abbey who acted as estate managers or bailiffs on behalf of their distant abbot. Some granges also incorporated a chapel in which an ordained member of the monastic community would say mass and administer the sacraments to the lay-brothers and the estate workers. Cockersand had granges at Pilling and Newbiggin (Little Singleton), in Amounderness. Other large holdings of the abbey, such as Medlar, in Amounderness, did not see the construction of granges and were probably run by bailiffs, as were manors we have mentioned like Westhoughton, Tarleton and Hutton. The large expanse of land in Preesall that was given in the early thirteenth century by the de Hackensall family lay immediately adjacent to Pilling, and was administered by the abbey as part of Pilling for more than three centuries. This led to confusion after the Dissolution when men resident in that part of Preesall, known as the Lower End of Pilling, claimed to be residents of Pilling and, therefore, not liable for service as watchmen or constables in Preesall.

Where a monastery such as Cockersand Abbey ran its own estates, whether as granges under lay brothers, or as manors under stewards or bailiffs, it required workers on the land. These were the same sort of people that provided the labour on any other estate. They were mostly unfree men – though not slaves – of the villein class: tied for the whole of their lives to the estate or manor on which they lived and worked. Where a manor was granted to a monastery, the people who lived on it were transferred with it. If a manor lacked people – the manor of Rossall on its transfer to Dieulacres Abbey, for example – a number of unfree men, *nativis*, as they were known, would be sent, donated like any other commodity, to make up a suitable labour force. We have records of considerable numbers of such people being given to Cockersand. For example, around 1265, Geoffrey of Hackensall gave to Cockersand one Adam, son of Jordan of Preesall, with all his brood and all his chattels both movable and immovable. In these circumstances a man's status depended on that of his father before him. If the father was a villein, then so too was the son.

During the thirteenth century there was a period of development and growing prosperity in England, which would have allowed Cockersand to make considerable use of its landed resources. By the early fourteenth century, however, a serious downturn in the economy had taken place and landholders, including monastic establishments, began to consider whether there might be greater profit in the letting of land than in the cultivation of it.

Population Greatly Reduced

Whatever abbots and other landholders might have thought on this matter, events of the mid-fourteenth century placed many of them in a position where, because of labour shortages, renting had become a very attractive option if tenants could be found. This situation was brought about by the Black Death which reached Lancashire in 1349 and, by early 1350, had reduced the population by as much as half in some areas. The labour shortage was made critical by further visitations of the plague, initially in 1361-2, 1369 and 1379, with as many as thirty separate outbreaks over the next century and a half. The effect of this on the rural economy was very great and some land that had been cultivated in the thirteenth century was lying idle in the fifteenth for want of men to work it.

Large-scale Letting of the Estates

Many landowners were letting large parts of their estates by the end of the fourteenth century and it is probable that the abbot of Cockersand was among them though we have no surviving documentary evidence for this. The first clear indication of large scale letting comes in the Cockersand Abbey Rental of 1451 which shows all the abbey's major estates, with the notable exception of Pilling, in the hands of tenants who were paying substantial rents. For example, the Amounderness estate of Medlar had four principal tenants, each paying £1 6s. 8d. per year, plus six hens. Interestingly, there are three further entries of the Medlar rents: 1461, 1501 and 1537 which show that the rent did not rise in almost a century, remaining exactly the same in 1537 as it had been in 1451. Little Singleton had four principal tenants in 1451: three paying £2 each and the fourth 13s. 4d.; a total of £6 13s. 4d.. By 1537 the number of principal tenants at Little Singleton had risen to five but the total of rent payable had risen by only fourpence to £6 13s. 8d.. At Singleton the poultry required as part of the rental was capons rather than hens. Similar situations can be observed with all the major Cockersand estates.

Although the first reference we have to large-scale letting of the major holdings is that of 1451, it clearly did not begin in that year. The rentals, by their extent and complexity, suggest that these represent long-standing arrangements, with tenants installed at a much earlier date. Words like: *uxor*(wife), *heres*(heir) and *filius*(son), all of which appear among the 1451 entries, point to tenants who held land before that date and had died, their holdings passing on to members of their families.

The Pilling Estate

Cockersand's first major holding – the manor of Pilling – was retained by the abbey as the home farm, and because it does not appear in the rentals just considered we do not know much of what went on there until the time of the great inventory of 1536. At the abbey's other manors, the crops, livestock and agricultural implements that were present when the inventory took place belonged to the tenants and so are not listed among Cockersand's assets. At Pilling, however, everything of an agricultural nature belonged to the abbey and so was listed and valued by the commissioners. This farm inventory is of considerable importance. We have little in the way of accurate information for stock and equipment of Lancashire farms of the period and the Pilling material serves as a reliable guide.

The first point to take the eye is just how little land there was under cultivation at Pilling in 1536; a year that presumably differed little in this respect from any other. There were three acres sown with wheat, ten with barley, two with peas and thirty-two with oats. The anticipated crops were valued at: wheat £1 10s., barley

£3 10s., peas 4s., oats £6 8s.. This is a small arable enterprise indeed and could not be compared in any way with some estates in the south of England: Ramsey Abbey in Huntingdonshire for example, which had thousands of acres under the plough and produced wheat and barley by the scores of tons. The agricultural equipment listed at Pilling is what we might expect for such limited cultivation. There were four wagons, twelve yokes and twelve iron chains, valued together at eight shillings. Three ploughshares and three coulters were said to be worth one shilling and eightpence, while two harrows with iron tines were worth one shilling each.

Neither pigs nor sheep were kept in any great numbers. Pigs were not normally kept in pens but were pastured in woodland, a feature lacking in the Pilling landscape. There were therefore only eighteen pigs of various types, valued together at £1 1s. 10d. Nor were sheep suited to the mossland of Pilling. Only on the salt-marsh could they find conditions to their liking but the numbers that could be pastured there were limited by the need to take them elsewhere when the marsh was covered by the tide. There were 87 sheep and lambs said to be worth a total of £4 9s. 0d. A few horses were kept and the commissioners noted ten of various ages: three old carthorses, two mares, two colts of two years and three of one year or less. The total value placed on the horses was £2 6s. 8d..

It was in cattle that the abbey was richest on its Pilling estate. There were twenty-four draught oxen at fifteen shillings each. This number represented three teams of eight which would have been used to cultivate the few fields of arable and also the smaller plots or strips worked by the abbey's minor tenants at Pilling. The milk-herd stood at fifty-eight, with a total value of £23. This would soon have been increased, however, as there were thirty heifers of three years which would shortly be producing calves and milk. Next on the list is an entry showing forty-two stirks of one year. The females would be in calf in a little over two years time and the males would go either for beef or draught oxen. Three bulls were kept and these were valued at seven shillings each which is interesting since the milk-cows were said to be worth eight shillings each. Selective breeding techniques of later centuries would surely have placed a much greater value on the bulls. Also listed were eighteen wild cattle which included two bulls and one calf. Wild cattle were still fairly common in the more remote parts of Northern England and sometimes appear in inventories such as this one. It is unlikely that any attempt was made to milk them but they would certainly have been used for beef and leather. A herd of wild cattle such as those listed at Pilling may still be seen at Chillingham in Northumberland. The total value of the cattle was reckoned at £45 6s. 0d. These were the cattle at Pilling that were owned by the abbey. The inventory does not list the cattle using the common pasture there and belonging to the tenants and estate workers.

The picture at Pilling would have been repeated on other estates, both lay and monastic, throughout Lancashire. The area may not have been well-drained and productive in arable crops but it did, and does, produce excellent grazing which allowed men to count their wealth in cattle and to derive much of their protein from the cheese for which the county has become noted.

The greater part of the abbey's activities at Pilling took place, of course, on a relatively small part of the manor. The arable and pasture was estimated in the sixteenth century at 1,000 acres: less than one sixth of the total. The rest was mainly moss, useful for fuel and little else. Animals could not be pastured on it and there does not seem to have been much in the way of rushes for thatch, fishing, or the annual migrations of wildfowl such as we find in the Fenland of Eastern England or the Somerset Levels. The salt marsh was a little more useful. Sheep, as we have seen, could be pastured when tide permitted and there would have been some wildfowl. It is unlikely that geese came in the winter on the same scale as they do now. Though they do eat grass, today's geese feed, where they can, on the rich root-crop and corn-stubble fields of the agricultural hinterland which were not present until relatively recent times.

Gifts of Other Kinds

Grants and gifts of other kinds were frequently made to religious houses. Cockersand received: mills, such as that of Greenhalgh in Amounderness c.1200; fisheries in rivers such as the Lune and the Wyre; rents, where a landholder simply transferred the rent rather than the land; annual sums of money; rights of pasture; rights of way; glandage; water rights; salt pits; turbary; the right to take timber, both standing and fallen; and perhaps most important of all, tithes: one tenth part of all produce in a township. Among the charters listed in the Cockersand Chartulary there are large numbers of grants and donations of these various kinds.

Churches were an important, and extremely valuable form of donation to monastic houses. In the middle ages a church or chapel was normally the property of the lord of the manor, and was his to dispose of as he saw fit. A church could provide a considerable income in the form of spiritualities: fees for such services as burials, marriages and baptisms, and temporalities such as rents and tithes. Particularly valuable was the tithe, which was in the gift of the lord of the manor and could be donated seperately or together with the church. Where a monastery received a church it usually appointed a secular priest as vicar. In the thirteenth century, however, disputes over control, between monasteries holding churches and the bishops of the dioceses in which the churches were situate, led to abbots and priors simply appointing their own men to these livings. This was particularly appropriate in the case of Augustinian and Premonstratensian houses as the canons were ordained priests. The practice was followed by Cockersand.

It is a little surprising perhaps that Cockersand Abbey held only two churches: Garstang and Great Mitton, not far from Clitheroe but on the Yorkshire side of the county boundary. Garstang church was the one that is now known as Saint Helen's, Churchtown. The present town of Garstang was seperately distinguished as 'market-town'. The parish church of Wigan was also given to Cockersand but the donation seems not to have been activated since it does not appear as one of the abbey's assets.

The financial value of such churches is amply illustrated in a dispute between the prior of Lancaster and the abbot of Cockersand in 1256. Because of its perceived sanctity and the piety of its canons, the new abbey on its bleak shore became a popular place of burial in the district. The prior of Lancaster complained to the archdeacon of Richmond, within whose jurisdiction such matters lay, that numbers of Lancaster folk, parishioners of the priory church, were opting for burial at Cockersand, thus depriving his church of the of the fees customarily paid for *sepulture*. Other sacraments were also being sought at Cockersand by Lancaster parishioners and the prior could see a considerable diminution of his church's income. The archdeacon delivered a judgement worthy of Solomon; any Lancaster parishioner could be buried, or take the sacraments, at Cockersand Abbey, provided he paid the appropriate fees to the prior of Lancaster.

Windows of the late thirteenth century when the Early English had begun to develop into the Decorated style; perhaps too late for Cockersand.

THE COCKERSAND COMMUNITY

The Daily Cycle of Prayer

As we have seen, the prime function of a religious house was prayer and intercession. This was carried on literally round the clock by the monks or canons who had dedicated their lives to to this very purpose. The central feature of a monastery was its church and in it the inmates spent a large part of every day participating in the *Opus Dei*, (Work of God). With a few variations, the monastic orders followed the same routine of attendance in church and the singing of the liturgy, or Divine Office, which involved all members of the community, collectively, at prescribed times throughout a twenty-four hour cycle. The first visit to the church was for Matins (originally known as Nocturns) which was at around 2am. Next came Lauds(formerly Matins) at about 5am. At first light came Prime, then Terce between 8 and 9am. and Sext at about 12.30, followed by sung High Mass, then reading. In late afternoon came Vespers and finally Compline in the evening after which the community retired in order to obtain a reasonable amount of sleep prior to rising for Matins. These times might be varied a little according to the time of year, indeed, Knowles points to a lack of any reference to actual times of day in the medieval monastic *horarium*. There were then, seven parts of the Divine Office together with High Mass, demanding the attendance in church of monk or canon. Also, for the Cockersand canons who were ordained priests, there was the requirement that each say Mass daily. This led to a situation in which the monk perceived the day quite differently from the layman or even the secular clergy. Where ordinary people tend to divide the day into morning, afternoon and evening, with night as a period of oblivion, the monk made no such division. His day was an endless cycle of prayer.

The Canons

The group of canons that came from Croxton to Cockersand to set up the new Premonstratensian priory will probably have numbered thirteen: twelve canons under a prior, named in early documents as Henry. We do not know exactly how many canons there were at Cockersand for most of the time in almost three centuries: from the foundation to about the last quarter of the fifteenth century. The greatest numbers are likely to have been in the abbey's early years when public enthusiasm, both for the order and for the new abbey, was at its highest level. In

1218 the Premonstratensian house of Tongland, in Kirkudbrightshire, Scotland, was founded from Cockersand which would have required thirteen canons, with presumably at least that number remaining at the mother-house, making a total at that time of twenty-six or more. During the fourteenth century the Black Death and subsequent outbreaks of the plague reduced the numbers and kept them low. In 1369 there were fourteen canons and in 1381 there were only thirteen.

It was during this period, in 1363, that Pope Urban V decreed, exceptionally, that any young canons at Cockersand who were not yet priests could be ordained on reaching the age of twenty-one to make up for the shortage of priests caused by the plague. In 1412 this concession was made permanent by Pope John XXIII because of the remoteness of Cockersand and the difficulty of finding men to serve there.

Occasional snippets of information have survived from the thirteenth and fourteenth centuries concerning individual canons. We have a document of 1327 which tells us that Robert de Hilton, canon of Cockersand, was pardoned for the death of Robert de Preston, lately a canon of the same house. Unfortunately we are told nothing about the circumstance in which the unfortunate canon met his death, nor why it was necessary for de Hilton to be pardoned. In 1387, William Spencer of Ormskirk, a canon of Cockersand, had conferred upon him the dignity of papal chaplain. A similar dignity was conferred in 1400 upon another of Cockersand's canons: Nicholas de Warton.

Canons Serving Away from the Abbey

The picture becomes clearer when we have reports made by visiting officials in the late fifteenth and early sixteenth centuries. These documents indicate a norm at that time of something around twenty canons belonging to Cockersand. Of these at least four would be living away from the abbey: the procurators of Great Mitton and Garstang, and the *cantors* of chantries at Tunstall and Middleton. At times there were six canons living elsewhere, for in addition to the procurators of the two churches, the abbey often provided the vicars also. At Garstang, for example, there would normally be five or six clergy who would be responsible for services: at Saint Helen's church itself and at the two chantries in the church: that of the Blessed Virgin Mary, built and funded by the Rigmaiden family, and that of Saint James similarly provided by the Brockholes family of Claughton. There were also several chapels within this large parish that were served by the Garstang clergy. These included: the chapel at Pilling, one at Claughton which is first recorded in 1338, and the chapel of the Holy Trinity in Garstang market-town, for the building of which a licence was obtained in 1437. The vicar, of the parish of Garstang, though often a canon of Cockersand, might sometimes be a secular priest appointed by the abbot, but there would always be one of the canons present as procurator to see to the running of such a large parish, the maintenance of churches and chapels within it, and to ensure that all dues and revenues were collected on time. We know several Cockersand canons who served as vicars of Garstang. Thomas Green was appointed around 1395 and left in 1410 on being elected abbot of Cockersand. Green must have lived to a considerable age as he was evidently still abbot in 1437. Canon John Bradford was vicar from 1481 to 1500 and Thomas Bowland from 1508 to 1515. The parish of Garstang was a valuable asset to Cockersand. At the time of the abbey's closure the value of Garstang church was assessed at £40, and it was clearly in the abbey's interests to have at least one of the canons permanently present.

Mitton church was a little less lucrative, but at £35 per annum it still represented a valuable asset to the abbey. There was a chapel at Waddington served from the church, a chapel at Bailey – within the jurisdiction of Mitton parish – and a chantry that was established there in 1339. Cockersand Abbey was involved in major litigation over its title to Mitton church. The abbey had been granted licence to appropriate the church in 1314, and this had been confirmed in 1341 by Edward III. However, in December 1367, a secular priest named Thomas Sotheron declared that on the death of the vicar, William of Tatham, in 1360, the abbey's title to the church had lapsed and he declared himself to be vicar. Together with his brother he came to the church with armed men and drove out Canon Richard de Burgh of Cockersand who had been appointed vicar by the abbot. In 1368 Sotheron made representations to the Pope in support of his position, and actually had himself inducted as Vicar of Mitton by the abbot of Whalley. The Cockersand community reacted strongly, both in court and in terms of physical action. One of the canons – unfortunately we do not know which one – turned up at Mitton with a body of armed men and forcibly expelled the usurper. We hear no more of Sotheron; the abbey was confirmed in its possession of Mitton and every vicar from then until the suppression of Cockersand in 1539 was a canon of the abbey.

The Canons' Origins

In the abbey's early days, a reference to the abbot or one of the canons is simply the man's Christian name since surnames had not come into use at that time. By the fifteenth century, however, surnames were in fairly general use and we find them in respect of the canons. A common form of surname was a person's town or village of origin, which is clearly the case among the majority of Cockersand canons and from it we learn just how local most of them were. If they came from the place after which they are named most of the canons were from within twenty-five miles of the abbey. In 1481 for example, out of nineteen canons listed we find most of them with names that indicate a nearby place of origin. The abbot was William Bowland, a name shared with one of the canons, there was a Milo Chatburn(near Clitheroe), John Bradford(near Clitheroe), John Bank(south of the Ribble near Tarleton), Hugo Fawcett(near Bury), Matthew Kirkby(there are several, probably Kirkby Lonsdale), Thomas Poulton(either Poulton le Fylde or Poulton le Sands[Morecambe]), Robert Singleton(in the Fylde), James Skipton(West Yorkshire), Henry Staining(Fylde), Robert Burton(two places within twenty miles), William Bentham(just inside West Yorks.), John Lancaster, William Hutton(probably the abbey's manor south of Preston), John Preston. Only John Woods, George Lyndsley and Edward Becroft have names that are not immediately recognisable as place-names fairly close by.

Of the twenty-two canons listed at the time Cockersand Abbey was dissolved, twenty-one had names that are unequivocally local place-names. They are: Robert Poulton, Richard Aldcliffe, Roger Claughton, Abiam Clitheroe, John Preston, John Holme, Edward Betham, Brian Furness, Edward Garstang, Robert Forton, Leonard Bentham, John Downham, Robert Caterall, Oliver Burton, Richard Preston, Thomas Dalton, Radulph Plumpton, Radulph Horton, William Whalley, Richard Sawley, Jacob Kirkland. The surname of the one remaining canon has been obscured.

Interestingly, the list of canons at Cockersand at the time of the litigation concerning Mitton church, which we have considered above, shows some of the canons to have been from much further afield in the fourteenth century. The date of this list is 1369 when the population was particularly low because of the ravages of the plague that had swept the country on a number of recent occasions. There were at that time only fourteen canons in place at Cockersand, including the abbot. Some were local, such as William of Preesall, John of Eccleston and Richard of Preston. However, at this date we find men whose names suggest much more distant places of origin than was normal in the fifteenth and sixteenth centuries. The list includes: Roger of Nottingham, Richard of York and Robert of Newark. The place of origin of the abbot, Jordan of Bosedon, is unclear. It could be Bowston in Westmorland, but it might equally be Boston, in Lincolnshire.

Many of those who entered the religious life were members of the aristocratic families that formed the chief military component of feudal society. A man of this class might expect to spend much of his life involved in warfare, or in preparation for warfare, on behalf of his king, but it was held that a man could fight for mankind with prayers and piety just as well as could his brother with sword or lance. A younger son, therefore, might find status and reward by entering a monastery when there was no inheritance for him from his father's estate. There is nothing, however, in the names we know from Cockersand to show that any of the canons were of the great families of the area and the likelihood is that these men were members of lesser landholding families in the various manors suggested by their names, or possibly sons of some of the abbey's major tenants. We can say with some confidence that they are unlikely to have been members of the villein, or unfree, class. Those from the lowest orders of medieval society could not have aspired to membership of a group largely recruited from the higher ranks. They would have lacked education and, most important of all, because they were unfree they required the permission of their lord of the manor before leaving it. The lord of a manor was not keen to give such permission as the successful running of the estate depended to a great extent on the labour available. He was not, therefore, likely to allow his labour force to be reduced by individuals going off to become monks.

Other Residents of the Abbey: Lay Brothers

Another group we find in monasteries is the lay-brothers, or *conversi*. Some of these men did come from the lower levels of society, though even here we find members of the manorial landholding families. The lay-brothers were lesser members of the order: men who did manual or menial work and were not allowed or expected to play a full part in the liturgical life of the monastery. Many were illiterate, or at best poorly educated. As a class they came into their own in the early years of the Cistercian movement, that is, the twelfth century, when some newly built abbeys found themselves with vast estates, and monks who were ill-suited by their background and calling to carry out the many tasks that such estates demanded. In any case, monks had much greater and higher demands placed upon them. They were there to pray, to carry out the *Opus Dei* which meant observing the liturgical cycle around the clock. So the idea of creating 'second-class monks' was seen as a means of having the heavy work done by men who were not servants or hired hands, but members of the order who could be relied upon to be loyal and diligent, though not required to attend church so often as the monks. As we have seen, in some Cistercian houses there were large numbers of lay-brothers, such was the popularity of the order. Many who joined were recruited by abbots specifically for the skills they had to offer. Masons were always in demand, as were carpenters, cooks, brewers, farriers, and those with knowledge of agriculture and stock rearing. A man of low degree who could get himself accepted as a lay-brother, even though that meant hard work and a life of celibacy, had brought about a considerable improvement in the material quality of his life and in his status within the general community.

Though the idea was so popular in its early days, there was soon a great fall-off in the numbers coming forward to be lay-brothers, while among those already in the monasteries there was, by the end of the twelfth century, a growing discontent. In some cases this became outright mutiny and occasionally an abbot needed to bring in soldiers to quell the riotous lay-brothers. Many abbots became reluctant to take in new *conversi* and they virtually disappeared as a class. For example, when the community of Cistercian monks moved from Stanlow Abbey, Cheshire in 1296 to found their new abbey at Whalley, their numbers included only one lay-brother.

The lay-brother was essentially a Cistercian institution, but the idea was soon adopted by other orders, including the Premonstratensians. This did not mean, however, that Cockersand Abbey, or any other Premonstratensian house, ever had them in the kind of numbers we have seen in some Cistercian houses. H.M. Colvin, the authority on the order in England, was able to discover very few of them in Premonstratensian houses. At Cockersand, only four lay-brothers can positively be identified as such. The first of these was called Richard and he appears in a document of 1251-60, by which he is shown to have received the sum of forty marks (one mark equalled 13s. 4d.) for payment to the parson of St. Michael's on Wyre, and fifty marks for disbursements, we are not told to whom. This brother Richard was possibly the *grangarius* of the abbey's grange at Newbiggin, as Little Singleton was at that time called. The grange was only a short distance from St Michael's church and village. Our second lay-brother occurs in a document of 8 July 1347, in which one John de Catterall complained to the justices that he was assaulted and maimed in Lancaster by Robert de Carleton, abbot of Cockersand together with four canons, John le Mason, lay brother of Cockersand, and fifteen further named individuals, plus others not named. It is difficult to imagine what the abbot was doing in Lancaster with more than twenty men at his back. Was he out looking for the victim, and what was the dispute about? The de Catterall family was a substantial landholding family in the district and the victim was a man of some local standing, and though the document gives us no details we might suppose it to have been over land, or rights of some kind. No land is recorded as having been given to the abbey in Catterall but in nearby Garstang and other adjacent manors, there was plenty. A likely reason is that John de Catterall was disputing the payment of tithes to Garstang church, which was, of course, appropriated to Cockersand Abbey. Equally, it could have been about grazing rights, a common bone of contention during this period.

Apart from Richard in the thirteenth century, John le Mason in the fourteenth, and two others who appear in the poll-tax return of 1380-1, we have nothing to show that Cockersand ever had lay-brothers at all. Indeed, it would appear that the grange at Pilling was under the management of a non-monastic steward or bailiff from an early date. In 1242 a composition between the Abbot of Cockersand and the Abbot of Leicester in respect of the Cockerham estate contains a reference to Henry the granger (of Pilling). Had Henry been a lay-brother he would almost certainly have been referred to as such.

Abbey Servants

A monastic house, even a relatively small one such as Cockersand, had a considerable number of servants, many of them resident. Unfortunately it is only at the end of the abbey's life, when the inventory of 1536 was made, that we learn something of these servants, their numbers and the tasks they performed. More than fifty servants are recorded, though not all by name. For example: Edward Holme and Robert Croskell are listed as 'hinds of husbandry', that is farm labourers, each of whom was paid £1 6s. 8d. per year. George Dickinson, malt maker, was paid £1 per year while John Dobson and John Ball, smith and miller respectively, received the same wage as the farm workers. William Redford, general labourer, and Robert Brade, ploughman, received no wages but were fed and clothed by the abbey. A number of others including George Harrison and William Bell, horse keepers, and Thomas Holme, overseer at Pilling, received the top wage along with the miller, smith and farm labourers. Two women are listed among the outdoor servants: Margaret Carver and Janet Harrison, winnowers of corn, who each received the sum of eight shillings and fourpence per year. A large proportion of the servants, thirteen in all, are not named but worked indoors in the bakehouse, brewhouse, kitchen, pantry and buttery. Collectively, the domestic group of servants received an annual total of £17 13s. 4d. in wages. This is the group among which we could have expected to find the women with whom some of the canons strayed from the observance of their priestly vows, and who had by this date been forbidden to enter certain parts of the abbey.

Any establishment, monastic or otherwise, of similar size to Cockersand would have expected to employ this number of servants, both indoors and out on the land. The total annual wage-bill at Cockersand in 1536 was £46 16s. 8d.

Charity

There were still more residents making demands upon Cockersand's limited resources. In 1536 fifteen further people, described as 'poor', were fed and housed at the abbey's expense. These fell into two distinct categories. The first group, five in number, was made up of people who were evidently *corrodians*, that is individuals who had paid in advance, rather in the form of an insurance policy, for board and lodgings at the abbey in their later years, and ultimately for burial within the precincts. John Trenchmore from Skerton was such an individual. He had paid ten marks, £6 13s. 4d., and when he took up residence at Cockersand he received a room with bread, ale, meat, fish and fuel for the remainder of his life. The annual cost to the abbey of John's residence there was £3 6s. 8d., a figure that may already have placed the abbey out of pocket on his behalf since he had made his payment in 1531, though we do not know when he took up residence.

Also living as corrodians were Robert Lowndes of Skerton and his wife Marie. They had made their agreement in 1529 but we are not told how much they had paid, nor when they took up residence at the abbey. Robert and Marie were provided with a house in which to dwell, with fuel for the fire, and received each week eight loaves of white bread and eight of grey bread, eight bottles of ale with victuals and meat daily from the kitchen, fish and flesh at noon and night and a milk cow kept the year round by the abbey. This provision cost the abbey £5 6s. 8d. per year. Ten of this group are said to have been kept by the abbey simply out of charity and are described as 'pore men'. The annual cost of maintaining these fifteen people was £22 7s. 4d.

Clearly then, Cockersand Abbey was home to a large number of people who lived in close proximity to each other out on that remote and windswept shore. Those of whom we know numbered almost one hundred, a figure that was probably exceeded on many occasions when visitors and travellers were afforded hospitality. The cost to the abbey of maintaining this number of people was clearly very high and abbots must often have been thankful that the house lay so far off the beaten track and that its inaccessibility kept wayfaring travellers seeking bed and board to a minimum.

Organisation and Discipline

The Premonstratensian order was centrally controlled, with supervision and inspection to ensure that the rites and practices of the order were properly carried out and that individual canons were conducting themselves fittingly. There was a General Chapter or meeting of abbots, under an Abbot-General, at which rules were made and standards laid down for the conduct of those within the order. All abbots were required to attend. In 1317, for instance, we find a document dated 10 August asking the constable of Dover Castle to allow the abbot of Cockersand to 'pass the sea at Dover" in order to attend the Chapter-General at Prémontré. This system gradually gave way to a federal or regional structure, with thirty-one seperate regions known as *circaria*. Under this arrangement, abbots and priors did not have to travel so far in order to attend meetings of their peers. In 1469 the Provincial Chapter was held at Leicester in the house of the Friars Minor, while that of 1476 was held at Lincoln, with the abbot of Cockersand and the prior of Hornby among the venerable fathers present. There was also established a system of visitation, or inspection, by which a senior abbot visited each priory or abbey of the order that lay within his jurisdiction.

Of early visitations at Cockersand we have no record and we are unable to say what the state of the house might have been. It is not until the last quarter of the fifteenth century that we have any indication as to how the community there was conducting itself. Our knowledge of this period comes from the visitation reports of Bishop Richard Redman, a senior member of the Premonstratensian order in England and Wales, who was abbot of Shap, and held succesively the bishoprics of St. Asaph, from 1471, Exeter 1495 and Ely 1501. Following his appointment as visitor of Premonstratensian houses Redman appeared at Cockersand for the first time in 1477, after which he made seven more visits at intervals of roughly three years.

The earliest of these reports indicates nothing untoward. On Redman's visit of 1478 a debt of £100 was reported, but this was soon paid off, and it is not until April 1488 that we receive indication that all was not well. On that occasion Redman came to Cockersand accompanied by Canon Robert Bedall, prior of Shap Abbey, who was a regular companion on inspectorial journeys. He reported that Cockersand was on the whole orderly and well governed, but he forbade the canons, on pain of excommunication, to reveal the secrets of the order or the plans of the monastery to great lords, or to use their influence to obtain advancement. The canons were also exhorted to be satisfied with their food, to attend all the services and not to wander about the country.

Two of the canons, John Barton and John Preesall, were found to be guilty of apostacy, and excomminicated. We are not told what the nature of their offence might have been, but it was evidently serious and presumably connected with the above warning concerning secrets of the order and plans of the house. Though excommunicated brethren were sometimes reinstated this does not seem to have happened with these two.

Serious Offences

In December of the same year Redman and Bedall returned to Cockersand to deal with a situation much worse than the one they had found in April. Redman opened his report on this occasion by stating that he had not for many years encountered such disgraceful behaviour. Canon William Bentham, who held the position of *cellarius*, was found to have been involved in a sexual relationship with a woman called Merioryth Gardner, an extremely serious offence delicately phrased in the report as a 'lapse of the flesh'. Bentham was ordered to perform forty days of penance and to be banished to Croxton Abbey in Leicestershire for a period of three years. Also charged with sexual incontinence was Canon James Skipton who held the positions of *granator* and *cantor*. He was said to have been involved with one Elena Wilson. Unlike Bentham, Skipton denied the offence and called upon his fellow canons to support him in his protestation of innocence. None would do so, and he was similarly ordered to undergo forty days of penance and to be banished to Sulby Abbey in Northamptonshire, not for three years like Bentham, but for seven years, the extra four years no doubt being imposed because of his claim to be innocent when everything pointed to his guilt.

Redman laid down some rules to prevent the recurrence of such scandalous conduct. For example he declared that there was to be no drinking of ale after compline and that no women were to be allowed in the infirmary, the refectory or the chamber known as the Jordan chamber, presumably because these rooms had been, or were likely to be, the scene of behaviour such as he had found it necessary to punish.

The banishment of Bentham and Skipton did not run its full course as prescribed by Redman. In April 1491, when the Bishop returned to Cockersand for his triennial visitation, the list of canons in residence shows Bentham holding the office of sub-prior, or third in charge, and Skipton as *cellarius*. If they left Cockersand at all they received considerable remission of their exile; more than four years in Skipton's case.

When Redman returned for his next visit three years later, he was presented with another serious case of sexual misconduct. This time it involved a senior member of the community, namely Thomas Poulton, formerly *cantor* of the chantry at Tunstall, but not shown in 1494 to be holding any position of authority. Poulton's scandalous behaviour involved two women: Margaret Ambrose and Alice Pilkington. As in earlier cases Redman ordered forty days of penance and banished the guilty canon to a distant monastery for three years; in this case Barlings Abbey in Lincolnshire. Also like the earlier cases, Poulton was quickly reinstated to a senior position at Cockersand. In 1497, the list of canons present at Redman's visitation shows Poulton holding the position of sub-prior.

Unlike Bentham and Skipton, who committed their acts of sinful indiscretion within the confines of the abbey itself, Poulton took advantage of his position at the

Tunstall chantry to form illicit liaisons away from the eyes of the community of canons to which he belonged. Nonetheless, he was clearly found out and was back at Cockersand under a cloud when Redman came on his visitation.

In 1497 there was no report of sexual misconduct but there was evidence of an atmosphere that was not as it should have been. The canons were enjoined to refrain from making opprobrious or scandalous charges against their brethren. They were also forbidden to draw knives upon one another.

Two of the canons, Robert Burton and Thomas Kellet, were removed from Cockersand in 1500, for reasons not made clear in the report, and a number of seemingly minor disorders were reported. Burton was subsequently restored to his place at the abbey, though Kellet was not. In fact, this particular record may be doing Thomas Kellet an injustice. Though removed from Cockersand he was clearly not long out of favour since the records of Mitton church show him as vicar in 1506, having been inducted on 9 June of that year. There were cases of disobedience to the abbot, canons lingering in bed when they should have been at matins, and some neglecting to attend services on the pretext of illness. Bishop Redman declared it inappropriate that canons should be making a practice of attending weddings, fairs and other secular assemblies. Also deplored were certain laxities in dress. Canons were forbidden to wear over their white habit a black garment with coloured streamers or tassels known as *liripipes*; and a particular form of footwear or slippers, favoured by some of the canons instead of the regulation sandals, was banned.

Most of the above would appear to be minor indiscretions on the part of men who had dedicated their whole lives to a regime that most others, even at that time, would have found intolerable. It was the visitor's responsibility, however, to identify these lapses, minor though they might appear, and correct them, so that the strictness and purity of the Premonstratensian way of life should not be modified or ameliorated in any way.

Though serious sins were sometimes revealed, the Premonstratensians were always ready to forgive even the gravest, and to reinstate the guilty ones in positions of trust and authority. James Skipton, is the best example of this. He fornicated, then lied about his guilt, and was banished from the house, but nonetheless became abbot and spiritual father of Cockersand only fourteen years later. In matters of forgiveness the Premonstratensians were following the precepts of Jesus. They could do no less.

THE END OF COCKERSAND ABBEY

When Henry VIII set in train the Dissolution of the English monasteries he was continuing a process begun on a small scale by Cardinal Wolsey as early as 1519. Wolsey had in mind the founding of colleges with the income of the monasteries he closed, but Henry was persuaded by his secretary, Thomas Cromwell, that the disposal of the religious houses and their landed property would realise a huge amount of money for the crown. A great inventory to determine the value of every monastery took place at Cromwell's instigation in 1535-6 and as a result many of the smaller houses were doomed to instant closure. The Act of Suppression was passed in March 1536, and under it, any house with an income below £200 was to be dissolved, a fate that befell more than 300 monasteries in that year. Cockersand's annual income was reckoned at £157 which placed it at immediate risk. The commissioners, however, gave the abbey a good report, and declared the income to be £282 which allowed it to remain in existence when all the other Lancashire houses were gone by 1538.

The Disposal of the Estates

The larger monasteries, and a few small survivers such as Cockersand, did not have long to dwell upon their good fortune at having escaped suppression. In 1539 some 250 houses remained, but by the end of the year all were gone. This final phase released vast estates to the crown which could be used as a source of income in the form of rents, or sold at their capital value to produce large sums of ready money. As we have seen, most of the estates were already let and the crown therefore had the immediate benefit of a large rental income no longer accruing to the monasteries. Most of the lands were eventually sold by the crown, but many not until long after Henry VIII was dead. Some of course were never disposed of and remain crown lands to the present day as part of the estates of the Duchy of Lancaster.

The estates of Cockersand were let(farmed), long before the abbey was suppressed, and the rental income, once the abbey was gone, went directly to the crown. Some of the lands were sold quickly while others remained in the possession of the crown for a considerable time. The site of the abbey itself, together with the demesne estate of Pilling, was sold to John Kitchen of Hertfordshire for the sum of

£700 8s. 6d. in 1543. Kitchen's eldest daughter, Anne, married Robert Dalton of Thurnham Hall and the abbey site passed into the Dalton Family who owned it for more than 400 years. The manor of Hutton was sold in 1546 to Laurence Rawsthorne of Berkshire for the sum of £560 2s. 6d., while Tarleton was sold by Edward VI in 1552 to Anthony Brown of Essex for £484 6s. 8d.. Many of the monastic estates, including those of Cockersand were sold to the sitting tenant as in the case of William Eccleston who purchased Little Singleton from the crown for £244.

The abbey's contents and possessions were quickly disposed of and the buildings demolished for the building material they provided. An engraving of 1727 shows the chapter house and a few fragments of wall; little more, in fact, than may be seen today. Local farm buildings and walls of the characteristic red sandstone are apparent round about; doubtless built with blocks taken from the abbey. These materials though, will have been used in a second or third rebuilding since no local structure appears old enough to have been built at the time of the abbey's suppression. Swarbrick, in 1923, refers to stones on the opposite side of the Lune evidently taken from Cockersand and also to windows in the Perpendicular style at Crook Farm, a little way up-river, which came, he believed, from the Cockersand Abbey steeple. These few, somewhat pitiful, objects are all that remain of an institution that once exercised enormous influence, not only in the immediate locality but over a very wide area.

The Fate of the Cockersand Canons

Cockersand's document of surrender to the crown was signed by the abbot, Robert Poulton, and all twenty-two of his canons, on 29 January 1539. The abbey offered none of the resistance that marked the end of houses like Whalley, Sawley and Cartmel. Recalcitrance in those houses had led to the execution of the abbots of the first two houses and some of the monks or canons of all three, with others being turned out onto the street to fend for themselves as best they could. This was not the fate that either the king or Thomas Cromwell had in mind for any of the monasteries. For those who surrendered their houses and estates quietly there were preferential livings in churches and cathedrals. Some senior abbots became bishops in the new dioceses established by Henry VIII, others became deans and archdeacons, while monks and canons regular filled many positions in the ranks of cathedral canons and parish clergy. For those who could not be found a suitable living, or chose not to seek one because of age or infirmity, there was a pension to be paid by the state. Pensions for abbots varied according to the size of the house in question. The abbot of a large Benedictine house might receive as much as £150 per annum, while the abbot of Cockersand is shown to have been allocated a pension of £40 per annum. Monks and canons could not expect anything so lavish as this but, nonetheless, were granted pensions of around £6 per year. Normally a former monk was not allowed to draw both a stipend from a clerical post and a pension from the crown, so it was clearly in the interest of the state to see that as many ex-monks as possible were found clerical livings.

The Cockersand documents show Abbot Poulton as being allocated his pension of £40, with twenty-one of the canons also to receive pensions of unspecified amount: probably £6. Little though this sounds we must bear in mind that the highest paid servants of Cockersand Abbey, probably married men with families to keep, received annual salaries of only £1 6s. 8d. in 1536. The canons then, with no-one to provide for but themselves, would have fared quite well on £6. The one canon who is not mentioned in the list of pensioners is Abraham Clitheroe, *custos* of the chantry at Tunstall. In that post he received an annual stipend of £6: as much as he would have received in pension, but he was living securely as a member of the household of Sir Marmaduke Tunstall at Thurland castle, and probably felt himself better off than he would have been with nothing more than his pension.

The oldest canon at the surrender of Cockersand had appeared in the list in April 1500 when Cockersand was visited by Richard Redman. It was noted then that of the twenty-two canons belonging to the abbey, nineteen were *sacerdos*, while the remaining three were not yet ordained. One of these three young men was John Holme, who would have been about twenty-four years old at the time of Bishop Redman's visit. In the survey of 1536 there appears a Canon John Holme, priest, 'aged sixty years and more'. He was now serving as procurator of Cockersand's impropriated church of Mitton. Holme was present to lend his support during this crucial survey of the abbey while two younger men: Abiam[sic] Clitheroe, aged fifty, and John Preston, aged fifty-two, serving in the chantries at Tunstall and Middleton respectively, did not put in an appearance. There might, of course, have been a dozen reasons why Clitheroe and Preston could not be at Cockersand to support their mother-house. Nonetheless, John Holme's presence suggests loyalty and fidelity as well as perception of the political realities of the day.

With the signing of the surrender the Cockersand canons, ordained priests to a man, disappear from our sight. No doubt most of them, particularly the younger ones, will have been found suitable livings that relieved the crown of the burden of their pensions. Perhaps we might be able to find a few of them serving in such posts in the decade or two after 1539, but it would be a laborious task, and an identical name serving as vicar of some church in Lancashire or Westmorland would not necessarily indicate that we had found one of our Cockersand men.

Neither do we hear any further of the corrodians and the 'pore' men who were in residence on the final day of the abbey's life. Though we know nothing of their fate, we can assume that they came to no harm since the crown gave an undertaking to meet all the obligations of the abbey, both in charity and in respect of those who had paid in advance for their retirement. They were failed in one respect, however. The corrodians had also paid in advance for their burial within the sacred precincts of the abbey, and this they were denied.

What Remains

The Cockersand Abbey site today is in many respects little different from the way it must have appeared to Hugh the Hermit when he came to set up his hospital more than eight centuries ago. The present day visitor experiences something of what Hugh will have found: on calm days, an empty remoteness and a tranquility broken only by the occasional call of the curlew, and on stormy days, the unbridled fury of the elements. Yet for more than 350 years this is not what it was like. People lived here; considerable numbers of them: Father Abbot, pious canons, serving girls, pensioners and old men living on charity, together with the farrier, the brewer, the maltster, farm workers, saddlers and grooms. Here was a living, thriving community set up to the service of God and for his glorification. These it achieved, and more, for in serving God it served his people. Who knows how many were maintained over three and a half centuries by the charity of the abbey? Who can say what benefits, both spiritual and temporal, were brought to the people of the area and of the parishes served for so long by the Cockersand canons? Never rich or prosperous, Cockersand Abbey maintained itself and fulfilled its obligations, both to God and to numberless folk in Lancashire and beyond, until quite suddenly, it was no more. A stroke of the pen took it out of existence, scattered its people and razed its buildings so that within a few short weeks all was gone, and the site of Askell's Cross had been returned to a condition that Hugh would have recognised.

There is no reference to baptisms at Cockersand, but these Norman fonts, c.1100-1200, show the variety of designs available when the church was built.

APPENDIX

Abbots of Cockersand Abbey

Though we know the names of very few canons at Cockersand during its lifetime of 350 years, we do have a fairly comprehensive list of abbots. This list has been compiled mainly from occasional references to individual abbots occurring in a variety of medieval documents. Many of these amount to no more than a single mention of a man, otherwise unknown, and give no indication as to the duration of his abbacy, or whether the man who follows him in the list was actually his successor. We have, for example, an abbot whose last reference occurs in 1340 and know of no other until 1347. The distinct possibility exists in such cases that there was one, or possibly more than one, between the two of whom we know.

William Farrer, **Cockersand Cartulary**, Vol. I, Part I, pp. XXI-XXIII, gives many of the references in which the names of the various abbots occur.

Hugh Garth, the hermit, said to have been first master of the Hospital before 1184
Henry, prior of the hospital, occurs in and before 1190
Thomas, 'abbas de Marisco' between 1194 and 1199
Roger, 'abbas de Marisco', then in 1205-6 'abbas de Kokersand.'
Hereward, appears in 1216 and 1235; (perhaps two different men)
Richard, one reference in 1240
Henry, various references between 1246 and 1261
Adam de Blake, occurs in 1269 and 1278
Thomas, *ditto ditto* 1286 *ditto* 1288
Robert of Formby, elected 1289, occurs 1290
Roger, occurs 1300
Thomas, elected c.1302, occurs 1305-7
Roger, occurs 1311, latest 1331
William of Bosdon, appears 1334-40
Robert of Carleton, occurs 1347, died 1354
Jordan of Bosdon, elected 1354, not mentioned for ten years,
 appears 1364-9
Thomas, occurs 1380
Richard, *ditto* 1382
Thomas, *ditto* 1386-9
William Stainford, occurs 1393

Thomas de Burgh, *ditto* 1395-1403
Thomas Green, elected 1410, occurs as late as 1436-7
Robert Egremont, elected 1444, occurs 1474
William Lucas, died 1477
William Bowland, elected 1477, died 1490
John Preston, elected 1490, occurs 1500
James Skipton, *ditto* 1502
Henry Staining, *ditto* 1505
John Croune, *ditto* 1509
George Billington, occurs 1520-22
John Bowland, *ditto* 1524-27
...... Newsham,
Gilbert Ainsworth, elected March 1531
Robert Kendall, *ditto* October 1531
Robert Poulton, last abbot of Cockersand; elected 1533, surrendered abbey 1539

More windows of the Cockersand building period.

GLOSSARY OF TERMS

ABBOT Superior of a monastery. The word means: father

AUMBRY A cupboard or locker in a church; often built into a recess

APOSTASY The abandonment of religious faith

APSE Rounded or polygonal recess in a building, often at the east end of a church

CANTOR, CANTATUS Chorister or singer

CAPITAL A section, usually decorated, at the top of a pier or column.

CELL A small monastic house that is not independent and is under the control of another monastery

CELLARIUS Monk or canon responsible for stores, particularly food and drink

CENSER Incense burner

CHAMBER A room within a building: usually taken to denote a bedroom

CHANCEL The part of the church, at the eastern end, containing the altar and choir. Often seperated from the nave by a screen

CIRCARIA Geographical regions into which the Premonstratensian order divided its houses for the purpose of inspection by visiting officials

COMPLINE The last service of the day: about 8 p.m.

CONVERSI Lay brothers

CORRODY Payment in advance for residence in a monastery in later life

CROFT A small field or enclosure: perhaps two acres

CROSSING The point at which the transept crosses the main body of the church

CUSTOS Warden

DEMESNE Part of a landholders estate set aside for his own use. It might be part of a manor or perhaps a whole manor as in the case of Pilling.

DISSOLUTION The closing of the English monasteries: 1536-39

DORTER Dormitory for monks or canons

FRANKALMOIGN A form of tenure by which monsteries held land in return for prayer

GLANDAGE Freedom to pasture pigs in woodland, from Latin glans, acorn; payment for this freedom is known as PANNAGE

GRANATOR Monk or canon responsible for supplies of grain for baking and brewing

GRANGARIUS Overseer of a monastic grange; originally a lay-brother

GRANGES Outlying manors or estates belonging to a monastery

HAY Sometimes rendered hey or hege. Has the meaning of: an enclosure. Used to denote a pasture or the hedge that encloses it. In the case of Pilling it refers to the whole estate

HIGH MASS Solemn service at which the celebrant is assisted by other clergy, choir and acolytes

HORARIUM The cycle of hours marking the daily offices or services

HUNDRED Administrative sub-division of a county; often called a shire

KNIGHT SERVICE A form of tenure in which a man held land in return for military service

LAUDS Praises: the monastic service following Matins

MATINS Monastic service formerly called Nocturns or Vigilliae

NATIVIS Villagers on a manorial estate who were not free men. There were various classes including: villeins, bordars and cottars

NAVE The western part of a church extending as far to the east as the choir or chancel. In a monastic church it was occupied by lay-brothers, abbey servants and members of the public

NOCTURNS Early name for monastic service held during the night. Also known as Vigilliae

OXGANG One eighth of a carucate: probably fifteen acres

PATEN Plate used at communion and as a cover for the chalice

PRIOR Second in charge of an abbey. Superior of a priory

PYX Box or receptacle for the sacred host, or wafer

PERPENDICULAR An architectural style c.1350-1530 that emphasised vertical lines

PISCINA A small recess, often highly decorated, set aside for the wine and water used at communion. Also a receptacle at the church door for holy water.

PRECEPTS Teachings, instructions

PRIME The office of the first hour, i.e. 6 a.m.

PROCURATOR Administrator responsible for buildings, finance etc.

REREDORTER Latrine

SACERDOS Priest

SANCTUARY LAMP A small lamp in a church which, when lit, indicates the presence of the Blessed Sacrament

SANCTUS BELL Rung at the most solemn parts of the Mass

SELLION A strip in a medieval common field

SEPULTURE Burial; also fees payable for this service

SEXT The office of the sixth hour, i.e. noon

TERCE The office of the third hour, i.e. 9 a.m.

TITHE One tenth of produce of the land; given compulsorily to the church

TOFT A cottage with a small area of land: perhaps one acre

TRANSEPT The part of a church that lies at right angles across the main body of the building

TRIFORIUM A loft or space above the side-aisles of a church, characterised by an elaborate arcade.

TURBARY The right to dig peat, or turf, for fuel

VESPERS The evening service in church or monastery

VILLEIN An unfree resident of a manorial estate

WINNOWER One who separates corn from chaff

A fine example of a door in the Early English architectural style c.1200-1300. The west door of Cockersand church may have looked like this.

Suggestions for Further Reading

Baskerville G., *English Monks and the Suppression of the Monasteries*, Jonathan Cape, 1937.

Colvin H.M., *The White Canons in England*, Oxford University Press, 1951.

Farrer W., *The Cockersand Abbey Chartulary*, 7 parts, Chetham Society, 1898

Farrer W. and Brownbill J., *The Victoria County History of Lancashire*, 8 vols., Archibold Constable, London, 1908

Knowles D., *The Religious Orders in England* 3vols., Cambridge University Press, 1969

Knowles D. and Hadcock R.N., *Medieval Religious Houses of England and Wales*, Longman, London, 1971

Midmer R., *English Medieval Monasteries* 1066-1540, BCA, London, 1979.

Raines R.S., *Cockersand Rental 1501*, Chetham Society, Manchester, 1861.

Southern R.W., *Western Society and the Church in the Middle Ages*, Penguin, Harmondsworth, 1970.

Swarbrick J., *The Abbey of Saint Mary -of-the-Marsh at Cockersand*, Lancashire and Cheshire Antiquarian Society Transactions, 1925.

All architectural designs depicted are taken from: *Styles of Architecture in England* by Thomas Rickman FSA, published in 1848. They are intended to show the kind of designs that might have been used in the church and buildings of Cockersand Abbey.

Column capitals of the time Cockersand was built.